More than a Farmer's Wife

More than a Farmer's Wife

Voices of American Farm Women 1910–1960

Amy Mattson Lauters

University of Missouri Press
Columbia and London

University of Missouri Press, Columbia, Missouri 65201
Printed and bound in the United States of America

5 4 3 2 1 13 12 11 10 09

Library of Congress Cataloging in Publication Data

Lauters, Amy Mattson, 1972–

More than a farmer's wife : voices of American farm women, 1910–1960 / Amy Mattson Lauters.

p. cm.

Summary: "Examining how women were presented in farming and mainstream magazines over fifty years and interviewing more than 180 women who lived on farms, Lauters reveals that, rather than being victims of patriarchy, most farm women were astute businesswomen, working as partners with their husbands and fundamental to the farming industry" Provided by publisher.

Includes bibliographical references and index.

ISBN 978–0–8262–1852–0 (alk. paper)

1. Women farmers—United States—History—20th century. 2. Women in agriculture—United States—History—20th century. I. Title. II. Title: Voices of American farm women, 1910–1960.

HD6077.2.U6L38 2009

338.1082'0973—dc22

2008056085

∞™ This paper meets the requirements of the American National Standard for Permanence of Paper for Printed Library Materials, Z39.48, 1984.

Designer and typesetter: Aaron Lueders
Printer and binder: The Maple-Vail Book Manufacturing Group
Typefaces: Baskerville, Bible Script T, Giddyup Std

In memory of Elsie Mae Coen Mattson

Contents

Acknowledgments

This work started long ago, at a Mattson family reunion, where campfire stories recalled life on the Mattson family farm and in the hunting cabin, and memorials to those family members who had passed before us showed up as food. We Mattson folks love to eat, and when we get together, depending on the season, certain foods have to be present. At this reunion, the summer after my grandmother passed away, fried chicken—her specialty—dominated a table packed with farm foods, and reminiscences about her life dominated conversation. The grief was still raw, and I yearned to help her be remembered.

Elsie Mae Coen Mattson was an extraordinarily strong lady, a respected pillar of her community, and a farm woman. Her influence on me and my choices is inestimable. And it was in thinking about her that I began to think about American farm women and their role in history. This book started there.

This work also owes much to my dissertation committee and mentors at the University of Minnesota: Hazel Dicken-Garcia, Nancy Roberts, Linda Jean Kenix, Linus Abraham, Elaine Tyler May, and Lary May. Their input and support helped make this project possible, and their influences on my thinking helped make me a better scholar. Financial support from the University of Minnesota School of Journalism and Mass Communication—including grant funds for photocopies and a dissertation proposal award that allowed me a summer off from teaching to write—also made this work possible. Thanks must be extended, too, to the Elliott School of Communication at Wichita State University, which offered financial support for the oral history project that bolstered the original research, and, in particular, to Patricia Dooley, Les Anderson, and Susan Huxman. (Les, you know more people than anyone else I know.)

Finally, thanks must go to the readers of *Country Woman* magazine, who generously opened their hearts to me, and to the other farm women who graciously shared their stories over coffee at their kitchen tables. This story belongs to you as much—if not more—than it does to me.

More than a Farmer's Wife

Introduction

My earliest memory takes me back to the farm.

I'm sitting in a high chair, fascinated by the tropical fish swimming in a massive tank just at my eye level. My grandma Elsie talks to me while she pulls a roasting pan, full of foil-wrapped ham-and-cheese sandwiches, out of her oven. The table in her farmhouse kitchen groans under its load of platters and bowls, filled to brimming with a variety of different foods.

In a prominent spot, "Gotta-go" casserole steams—a concoction made from everything left in the pantry and refrigerator that could still be eaten. Within minutes, the kitchen fills with big people, laughing, talking, and eating, and Grandma puts small pieces of a ham-and-cheese sandwich on the tray in front of me.

The memory fades there. I can't recall what happened next, nor did I, until recently, understand the significance of the memory. But I can see, as clearly as if I'd visited yesterday, the blue-and-white space and bustling activity of Grandma's farm kitchen.

When I focused on that memory at a family reunion in 2005, my father's eyes took on a little shine. "That must have been the day of the farm auction," he speculated. "You weren't more than a year old, but Mom had you in the kitchen while the rest of us worked outside."

Without realizing it, I had tapped a memory that is emblematic of the farm experience in the United States of the twentieth century. My grandfather's health was failing; my grandmother could not manage the farm, be his caretaker, and keep her job at the hospital. It was time for the couple to retire.

But none of their six sons wanted the family farm.

The farm, located in northern Wisconsin, was too much work, my cousin Jerry, the oldest of the cousins, told me when I visited him in San Jose, California, in 2006. He spent the summers of his youth working on the farm for our grandparents and after high school graduation became the first of the Mattson grandchildren to get a college degree, in electrical engineering. Jerry moved to California to work for a technology company. His father, Jim, the oldest of the six sons, owned his own farm in Minnesota but also worked for years in his local post office. Uncle Jim had served in Korea and was eighteen years older than my own father, Randy, the youngest of the Mattson boys.

The second son, Terry, moved to the Twin Cities area in Minnesota to work in a factory after his own military service. Uncle Steve followed his work to Denver, Colorado, before moving back to Wisconsin in the 1980s and dying, too young, of a brain aneurism. Uncle Dave served in the military during the Vietnam War years and returned to work as an electrician in different Wisconsin communities. Uncle Dan went to school at the University of Wisconsin–Madison on an ROTC scholarship, getting a bachelor's degree so he could work in the health care industry. My own father married at nineteen and spent the first decade of his married life working in various blue-collar jobs. It was the 1970s; economically, times were hard for folks in rural Wisconsin. Before he was thirty, my father had moved himself and his family to a larger, more populated community in central Wisconsin—the Chippewa Valley—and times began to get better.

None of them had wanted the farm. None of them had wanted the sweat and the worry, the work and the heartache, the faith and the pain it required to be a farmer.

They were not alone.

From 1910 to 1960, the number of rural and farm families in the United States declined by a third. Many farm residents fled to cities or more urban areas to achieve an education, a living, or both. At the same time, the number of people living in cities swelled, in part due to this migration of farm families, but also due to immigration from other countries to American cities. In 1910, more than half of the U.S. population lived on farms or in rural areas; by 1960, 69 percent of the population lived in urban areas. This demographic shift, as yet not fully explored or discussed, dramatically affected the social boundaries and expectations of the people who lived through it. For when the farmer's children went to the city, they took their values with them. And the ideology instilled by their upbringing clashed with that of the urban dwellers. This clash can be documented through popular culture; it can also be seen in the everyday lived experiences of farm families. This clash is one finding of this work, which explores, in particular, the roles of farm women in the United States during the peak years of this shift, 1910 to 1960.

Why farm women? I began to think about the centrality of farm women to the American rural experience very early in my doctoral program. Elsie Coen Mattson, my Grandma Elsie, passed away just before I started graduate work in the University of Minnesota's School of Journalism and Mass Communication. As I took seminars in varied classes in American studies, history, women's studies, and rhetoric, I explored what it meant to be a farm woman, a working-class woman, a rural woman, and a farmer's wife. I listened to the music popular with these women; I read the magazines and newspapers directed toward them; I read their diaries and their letters to the editor. I investigated the fundamental formation as a farm woman of my favorite author—Laura Ingalls Wilder—and got acquainted with the writings of her daughter, Rose Wilder Lane, who also shares a life story emblematic of the twentieth-century experience. This book began as a dissertation that examined the constructions of American farm women in six central national magazines directed toward them: *The Farmer's Wife, Farm Journal, Country Gentleman, Saturday Evening Post, Ladies' Home Journal,* and *Good Housekeeping.* That research is bolstered by oral histories collected from more than 180 women from across the country who were raised on or lived on farms during the years 1910–1960. This book is first and foremost a work of recovery; these are women whose voices are in danger of being lost to history.

What I found as I studied the magazines, talked to farm women, and read their unpublished diaries and memoirs was that farm women were fundamental to the farming industry. They were the backbone of the family business, the managers of the farm home, and the primary contributors to farm publications. Many were farming boosters, pledging eternal optimism about their businesses; others were not. I also found that a cultural gap between the lived experiences of urban women and rural women, already present in 1910, grew and solidified as the country underwent catastrophe and change, until by 1960 urban women and rural/farm women had virtually nothing in common: no common language, no common ideology, no means of communication that made sense to either party. Essentially, the greatest barrier to communication between these two groups of women was cultural; each side viewed the other through a distinct lens. Urban women considered farm and rural women to be uncouth victims of patriarchy and poverty; farm women considered urban women to be frivolous and lazy because they didn't work for a living.

Farm women always worked—inside their homes, inside their barns, outside in the fields, and outside in the community when it was necessary, and it often was. Women who gave up their autonomy as businesswomen traded a life of work and independence for the chance to live off their husbands' work in a luxurious city lifestyle. Such women were anathema to the rural experience. While the real advantages of city living were often discussed in the magazines studied here, occasionally with some longing, most women appeared to choose to maintain a business partnership with their husbands, and preferred it to the apparent luxury that could await them in the city. In private conversations and in correspondence with women who were born, raised on, or running farms between 1910 and 1960, the magazine constructions were borne out, to a point: many looked back on those years with longing and nostalgia, but also with the clear-eyed remembrance of hard work and difficult living conditions in some areas that prompted more than a few born on farms to seek other employment or options when they reached adulthood.

More than a Farmer's Wife?

A photo taken by Dorothea Lange in the midst of the Great Depression shows a young woman, Florence Thompson, old before her time, with a baby in her arms, a child hanging on her neck, and her hair pulled back. Her clothes are worn; her face is lined. She is careworn, a victim of poverty living in a patriarchal system in which she is a primary caregiver in harsh conditions. A symbol of conditions the Dust Bowl wrought on a generation of farm and other rural American families, the woman has become also a lasting symbol of what it meant to be a farmer's wife during the Great Depression of the 1930s.

The woman in Lange's photograph has become an iconic image of the American farm woman. But a very different image of farm women dominated the pages of *Farm Journal, Country Gentleman,* and *The Farmer's Wife* during those Great Depression years. The magazines' stories about farm families featured attractive, healthy young women and children, pink-cheeked and strong, and it depicted farm women as keepers of the farm home and equal partners in the running of the farm business. In this representation of the farm woman, she is happy, healthy, and strong. She works hard, but she has much to show for her work. Her family and her community respect her as much for her opinions on local, national, and world affairs as for her apple pie recipe and her needlework.

"Migrant Mother," photo by Dorothea Lange, 1937.

The disparity in the construction of these images—the American farm woman as victim or as independent and happy—arises from the differing values and realities of the cultures that created them. The tension between these two cultures and constructions—broadly, though problematically, identified as "urban" and "rural"—can be readily identified through popular culture and media from 1910 to 1960, and remnants of it exist yet today. As late as 2006, for example, the character of Martha Kent, mother to Clark Kent/Superman in DC Comics, was depicted in the movie *Superman Returns* as a worn-down victim of hard life on her rural Kansas farm. Yet, it must be noted, Martha Kent raised the man who would become a superhero, demonstrating her centrality to the legend and identifying rural values as the bedrock of truly American principles.

How were farm women presented in media and in their own writings across this fifty-year period of great change affecting women and farming? On the assumption that studying the media that directly addressed farm women as an audience and published farm women's writing might help answer these questions, I examined constructions of farm women in farm magazines and a wide variety of other sources. These sources reflect a paradox about how farm women were viewed in American culture—as victims of hard work and poverty who, conversely, were well respected in business—as well as prevalent views about farm life, the farm, and the men and women who remained on farms in a culture that was increasingly urban. These sources also reflect a substantial change in how farm women were viewed and constructed in mainstream publications over time. The division between urban and rural women, noticeable in 1910, widened over the fifty-year period. It seems likely that neither group could relate well to the issues of the other by 1960, even though all women were being treated in substantially the same way in the publications studied. Politically, in 1910, women in the United States were campaigning for suffrage, which they gained in 1920. The year 1960 was marked with continued discontent among women and heralded what has come to be called a second women's movement.

Farm Women in American History

Most histories of American women of this period treat them as a monolithic group, and what is written is dominated by the struggle for suffrage. Until relatively recently, little scholarship attended to differences among women—whether in demographics, interests, daily lives, or even race and class. In addition, despite the fact that farm culture dominated American society until at least the Civil War and that women were central to that society—and, hence, to the shaping of American culture—very little scholarship has focused on the American farm woman.

Neither the significance of farm women in American history nor that of the farmer to U.S. politics can be understated. At the country's founding, Thomas Jefferson envisioned a nation of small, self-supporting farmers in what has come to be called the agrarian ideal. Philosopher Paul B. Thompson notes that, in Jefferson's time, this agrarian philosophy evolved from an anticommercial, medieval natural law tradition to a libertarian conviction in the "absolute noninterference in the individual's rights to control the use of land."[1] This conception of noninterference remained a force in American ideology throughout the nineteenth century, even though government initiatives offered significant support to farming. In 1862 alone, government initiatives included the passage of

1. Thompson, "Agrarianism as Philosophy," in Paul B. Thompson and Thomas C. Hilde, *The Agrarian Roots of Pragmatism*, 32.

the Homestead Act, which gave free land to small farmers moving west; the implementation of the Land Grant College Act, which provided a college in every state to teach agriculture and mechanic arts to farmers' sons; and the formation of the U.S. Department of Agriculture (USDA), which recognized a need for a center to organize the concerns of what was at the time the major economic interest group.[2]

As the twentieth century dawned, tensions between industry and agriculture became more pronounced; as Thompson and Thomas Hilde note, agrarianism became "a form of populism and/or progressivism—and often reactionism—engaged in a reexamination of the notions of democracy, individual freedom, and cultural countenance of the coming America."[3] Agricultural communities were beginning to lose their populations to urban areas that many saw as offering more social and economic opportunities. According to the U.S. Census Bureau, in 1910 more than 32 million people lived on 6.3 million farms, which at the time was nearly 35 percent of the U.S. population. In 1960, 13.5 million people lived on 3.7 million farms, comprising 7.5 percent of the U.S. population.[4] This loss of rural population, a source of significant

Table 1. Percentage of U.S. Population by Rural or Urban Location

Year	Percent Urban	Percent Rural
1910	45.6	54.4
1920	51.2	48.8
1930	56.1	43.9
1940	56.5	43.5
1650	64.0	36.0
1960	69.9	30.1

Source: U.S. Census Table 1, "Urban and Rural Population 1900–1990," U.S. Census Bureau, October 1995. Online: http://www.census.gov/population/www/censusdata/files/urpop0090.txt (accessed December 2008).

2. Bushrod W. Allin, "The U.S. Department of Agriculture as an Instrument of Public Policy: In Retrospect and in Prospect," 1098.

3. Paul B. Thompson and Thomas C. Hilde, "Introduction: Agrarianism and Pragmatism," in Thompson and Hilde, *The Agrarian Roots of Pragmatism,* 4.

4. See Vera J. Banks, "Farm Population Trends and Farm Characteristics," Washington, D.C.: U.S. Dept of Agriculture, Economics, Statistics and Cooperative Service, 1978; Carolyn Dimitri, Anne Effland, and Neilson Conklin, "The 20th Century Transformation of U.S. Agriculture and Farm Policy," Economic Information Bulletin No. 20, Washington, D.C.: U.S. Department of Agriculture Economic Research Service, 2008.

concern to farmers, even as farmers gained political power with the government initiatives that backed them, is well documented.[5]

The history of the U.S. Department of Agriculture, formed in 1862, demonstrates the centrality of the farming industry to American culture and economics and underscores the country's Jeffersonian emphasis on the agrarian ideal. The political power of farmers rose with the 1867 formation of the Grange, a farmer's organization that eschewed Wall Street monopolies and special privileges in favor of free competition and enterprise. As Bushrod W. Allin wrote in 1960, the first fifty-eight years of the USDA's existence were marked by policies that underscored the concept of "economic orthodoxy"; that is, farmers worked within an economic framework that promoted capitalism. During World War I, from 1914 to 1918, the prices of farm products soared, and farmers in 1917 turned profits that were as much as 20 percent above the 1910–1914 averages. After the war, prices fell, and a second period followed during which agribusiness farm leadership was promoted by farmers. Allin identified this period, from 1920 to 1932, as one of temptation and indecision, characterized by the 1929 formation of the Federal Farm Board. The third period identified by Allin, from 1932 until the time of his writing in 1960, was one of economic and political power for the USDA and for farmers. The onset of the Great Depression in the early 1930s had eroded public confidence in business leadership, and Henry A. Wallace, the former editor of *Wallace's Farmer,* led a controlled farm production movement culminating in the passage of the Agricultural Adjustment Act in 1933. Such initiatives as price support for selected farm operations and crops grew out of that movement and the New Deal initiatives of the Franklin D. Roosevelt administration. By 1960, the USDA had taken on two primary tasks: improving farm productivity and strengthening farmers' economic and political bargaining power.[6] Allin wrote:

> Today, many of our farmers say they want family farms, free prices and a minimum of government action. But they must try to achieve these goals under entirely different conditions from those which confronted Jeffer-

5. See Allin, "An Instrument of Public Policy," as well as David Freshwater, "Farm Production Policy versus Rural Life Policy," and Sam B. Hilliard, "The Dynamics of Power: Recent Trends in Mechanization on the American Farm," as examples.

6. Allin, "An Instrument of Public Policy," 1099–1102.

> son and his followers. They are faced with an over-expanded agriculture which is relatively much smaller than the rest of the economy. The land is not free; it is not only all owned, but is also high in price. Farmers are not now largely self-sufficient; they produce mainly for sale. These are the reasons why the Department [of Agriculture] performs functions today undreamed of by its founders.[7]

Geographer Sam Hilliard, writing in 1972 about the increasing mechanization of farms during the previous thirty years, noted that mechanization had spurred the trend begun around 1910 and continuing to 1964 of a decline in the number and increase in the size of farms being operated. He argued that technological advances had helped spur this trend, but he said that, economically, farming was becoming more about big business than about family farming.[8] Economist David Freshwater, in examining more recent political power of farmers, wrote in 1997 that farm power "derives from a time when farm numbers were large, the plight of farmers was clear, and considerable public support existed for an active role for government." That support for farmers, he argues, continued to exist well into the 1950s because so much of the U.S. populace—including those who had moved to urban or suburban areas—still maintained family connections to farms. Farmers' retention of political power, he suggests, also came from their assertion that agriculture is the "economic motor" of rural areas. "The farm lobby developed its power at a very different time, and it could be argued that the last sixty years have been a brilliant example of how to maintain influence while gradually facing a loss of power."[9]

Thus, the political power of farmers in the United States, a country founded on an economic system that depended on farming, underwent significant change in the twentieth century. Changes in public policy, technology, and industry responded to population shifts from rural to urban areas, allowing the creation of large, big-business farms and driving some small farmers out of business.

What is known about farm women during those years? Written histories of farm women suggest that the available information may be skewed by the articulateness of a few of the women who rejected farm life, and thus the work of historians who rely on the writings of

7. Ibid., 1103.
8. Hilliard, "Dynamics of Power," 5.
9. Freshwater, "Farm Production Policy," 1516, 1518, 1519.

those women also may be skewed. Much scholarship assumes a need for change among women on farms, and it is possible that such assumptions stem from the negative perceptions of farm life provided by those who rejected it.

Historian Joan M. Jensen begins her collection of essays on farm women's history by tracing her own history as a farm woman. She discusses her experiences on a communal farm in 1970 and shares the story of her mother, who was born into poverty on a farm, ran away to the city in 1918, and refused to live on a farm ever again. "I share this family history," Jensen wrote, "because I feel that we must begin to study the history of farm women with our own past. Every woman has a farm woman in her family and most of us do not have to go back far to find that woman." Jensen also cites the numbers of prominent women throughout history who began life as farm women, adding that many of them rejected farm life as adults.[10]

Women who remained on farms took on varied roles, both on and off the farm. Rachel Ann Rosenfeld, in tracing patterns of farm women's work, shows that while farm women's roles may not have changed over time, the historical awareness of those roles may have changed. Official government attention to American women's roles on farms began to be paid as early as 1915, when the U.S. Department of Agriculture published a series of reports on farm women's social, labor, domestic, educational, and economic needs. Four other USDA studies were published in the 1920s; other USDA research in the 1930s examined women in the "hard times," and USDA studies in the 1950s and 1960s examined the work of farm wives.[11] Rosenfeld suggests that the reason for the USDA's interest in farm women is the value of their roles as producers of food and other commercial products that provide family income.

Women's labor history offers insights applicable to farm women's work, but very little has been published about women's farmwork as labor history. Discussing the value of women's work on the farm, Carolyn E. Sachs, in her 1983 labor study, addresses the "invisibility" of farm women's work, adding that women who engage in farmwork share a status with many urban women who also work outside their homes. Alluding to the problem of cultural patriarchy in farm production, she wrote, "There is still a strong tendency to see men as farmers and women

10. Jensen, *Promise to the Land: Essays on Rural Women,* 74, 81.

11. Rosenfeld, *Farm Women: Work, Farm, and Family in the United States,* 19.

as farmer's [*sic*] wives." She added, "Whether or not women engage in field work, they are still expected to have the major responsibility for child rearing, food preparation, laundry, and general housework."[12]

Historian Alice Kessler-Harris, who has written three books on women's labor history, alludes to—but does not elaborate on—women's work on farms, noting that the subject signifies a gap in labor history.[13] Labor history has focused on women's roles in urban and suburban areas, women's engagement with working-class politics, and class tensions between women of different classes and races over time. In her *In Pursuit of Equity,* Kessler-Harris has also studied legislative, policy, and court decisions that affect women in the paid, urban workplace.

Given the significance of farmers as a political bloc and of farming to the business structures of the United States between 1910 and 1960, the absence of scholarship surrounding farm women during this critical period is even more striking. Given that most contemporary American women can claim a farm woman in their ancestry, the fact that no one has yet questioned that influence also is striking. In this book I hope to address that gap and cast doubt on existing assumptions about farm women's roles. Using cultural studies theories, which assume media play a significant role in the shaping of culture and identity, I studied farming magazines and women's magazines as sites through which some of the history of this influential group of women may be recovered. Additionally, more than 180 North American women who were raised on or lived on farms from 1910 to 1960 shared their stories via interviews and correspondence; their voices helped me to explore how closely American farm women's lived experiences matched those constructions found in the magazines studied here.

From 1910 to 1960, sweeping changes in American culture directly affected all the country's citizens. The period encompasses two world wars, a severe economic depression now known as the Great Depression, a cold war struggle marked by the threat of nuclear annihilation, and political acts that included the granting of suffrage to women, Prohibition and its attendant legal challenges, and the development of the New Deal. Advances in technology also changed farming through this

12. Sachs, *Invisible Farmers: Women in Agricultural Production,* xi, 82.

13. See Kessler-Harris, *Women Have Always Worked, In Pursuit of Equity: Women, Men, and the Quest for Economic Citizenship in 20th-Century America,* and *Out to Work: A History of Wage-Earning Women in the United States, 20th Anniversary Edition.*

period, making self-sufficiency and survival less important than turning a profit; new farm machinery, electricity, telephones, and improved farming techniques often made the difference between survival and financial success. A burgeoning consumer culture, which can be traced through the magazines studied here, lured men and women into thinking success should be measured by an accumulation of goods; farming as a business was not always successful enough to compete with the lures of a paycheck in the city that could purchase those goods.

Understanding how farm women were constructed as women, citizens, and farmers through mass media from 1910 to 1960 may help scholars to understand how these women might have influenced succeeding generations. In the 1960s, the culture of the United States exploded with tensions that led to sweeping political movements such as the civil rights movement and the second wave of the feminist movement. Soldiers returning from their tours in Korea and Vietnam went back to school using funds from the GI Bill, and college attendance became an attainable goal for many working-class Americans. Mass media were central to the upheaval, as historian Godfrey Hodgson noted:

> The mechanism by which this question of the moral nature of American society came to obsess the nation's political attention from the time of the Kennedy administration on, was the media. Just as the media, by their coverage of civil rights and then of the war, had been primarily—if largely unintentionally—responsible for raising grand questions of morality in the first place, so, too, it was the media that led the retreat. There was nothing mysterious about what happened. Mass media are ultimately dependent on communicating with masses of people. In 1968 the mass media were abruptly reminded of the existence of the mass of ordinary working Americans and their families, of that majority that had been, for a decade, not so much silent as ignored.[14]

The concept of freedom in the 1960s was redefined and contested, as cold war ideology "highlighted the danger to liberty from excessive government," as historian Eric Foner wrote in 1998. At the same time, he added, "civil rights activists resurrected the vision of federal authority as the custodian of freedom."[15]

14. Hodgson, *America in Our Time,* 368.
15. Foner, *The Story of American Freedom,* 279.

How, then, might farm women have influenced these changes and philosophies? Throughout this book, the voices of women who were raised on or lived on farms from 1910 to 1960 provide a touchstone for reminding readers that history lives. Interviews and correspondence yielded a great number of stories, some of which aligned with media constructions of farm women and some of which did not. Women born on unsuccessful farms appear to have been more likely to choose to leave them as soon as they were able; women who ran their own farms continued to take pride in their work. All agreed that women worked hard on farms, and the general attitude can be wrapped up in what one woman told me: "It was a hard, but simple life," Joyce Kollars wrote. "And I feel we had more of a family life than anyone else has today."[16]

16. Joyce Kollars, memoir, 2007.

1

A Sense of Place
Farm Women in History and in Theory

A Kansas lawyer wrote to me in January 2007 about his willingness to share his mother's story for this work. "I . . . told her that I would suggest that she sit down and write all the detail she could think of about life as she remembers it. She did not think anyone would be interested," Randall Weller reported.[1]

This notion—that no one would be interested in their history—made it a challenge, in some respects, to elicit stories about farm life and farm roles from women who lived through the experience. The question, for some, was flattering; for others, it was strange and out of place. Women's lived experiences, they seemed to think, were nothing out of the ordinary. Why would any scholar be interested? In articulating this idea, these women reinforced a commonsense construction of women's history as unimportant, a construction that met limited challenges before the midtwentieth century.

Women's History

The study of women's history as a discipline developed relatively recently. The second wave of the feminist movement in the twentieth century included a generation of women scholars who, having noted the systematic suppression of the history of women's contributions to varied societies over time, engaged increasingly in research about women of the past. The problem, as historian Joan Wallach Scott has noted, was one of women's "invisibility"; history as a discipline was dominated by recitations of political milestones and discussions of the "great men" who brought them about.[2] Women were left out of such historical narratives.

1. Weller, email to author, January 3, 2007.
2. Scott, "The Problem of Invisibility."

Thus, the careful recovery of women's history was the primary goal of women's historians, whose work continues to develop an understanding of women's roles in history. The primary metaphor for describing gender roles was separate spheres, a doctrine articulated by historian Barbara Welter in 1966.[3] According to the separate spheres gender norm, women were confined to the sphere of home and domestic work, leaving the public sphere and civic life to men.[4] This idea that women and men were to work in separate spheres provided a starting point for many researchers to understand gendered history. A number of scholars have contributed to debates about the separate spheres ideology. Gerda Lerner, for example, noted that it applied primarily to middle- and upper-class women; furthermore, she asserted, the availability of working-class women to do work that middle- and upper-class women would not have to do in an industrialized society made it possible for such a class association to exist.[5]

Scholars have raised questions about race, class, and religion in relation to women's roles in society and have stressed the need to acknowledge the diversity of women's experiences. Still, much of women's history continues to focus on the urban woman to the neglect of the rural and farm woman. Despite the predominantly patriarchal culture of farming in the United States, farm women's roles were not confined to the home; farm women were expected to be partners with their husbands in the running of the farm business. But even though that partnership meant that women were not confined to the farm home, it did not protect them from the vagaries of the industrialized age. In important ways, farm women were working women. They were also social citizens in their rural communities,[6] and they expected respect for their work. The woven plaid used by Laurel Thatcher Ulrich to explain the public and private life of midwife Martha Ballard in eighteenth-century Vermont might be a fitting metaphor for farm women's roles: domestic life is one

3. Welter, "The Cult of True Womanhood."

4. Linda Kerber, "Separate Spheres, Female Worlds, Woman's Place: The Rhetoric of Women's History."

5. Lerner, *The Lady and the Mill Girl: Changes in the Status of Women in the Age of Jackson* (Andover, Mass.: Warner Modular Publications, 1969).

6. A "social citizen," as I have used the term here, is one who participates in daily civic and communal interactions with others in a given community, exercising power through social influence, rather than through political activity.

color, and civic life is another.[7] These are so woven together that, at times, they are inseparably blended. Neither role is isolated, but both are equally important to the overall pattern of farm women's lives.

A Cultural Approach to History and the Role of Mass Media

Historian Warren I. Susman, in *Culture as History: The Transformation of American Society in the Twentieth Century,* defined cultural history by saying that historians had too long focused on history as a succession of wars, politics, and record-keeping. This emphasis, he said, was void of the central experiences of history and the knowledge that could be gained from understanding the people who were affected by events. "To propose an examination of cultural history is to seek another understanding and to fulfill another mission," Susman wrote. Cultural history includes understanding and appreciating the tensions and convergences of ideologies in different cultural forms—such as "popular" culture and "high" culture—in an attempt to understand a cultural whole. "Because cultures are constantly in tension, because history is a fundamental part of culture, because being itself is essentially a contradiction, the dynamic of this historical process is composed of the working out of these tensions." Such tensions are worked out not merely in the classroom, where debates over the nature of the past as applied to present political problems are common, but also in the streets, taverns, and homes of everyday life, Susman argued.[8]

Historian Benedict Anderson pinpoints mass media as an important site for studying such everyday cultural tensions. Anderson, who suggests that national identity would not exist without the power of mass media to create an imagined community, says that the newspaper itself is a cultural product that links citizens by virtue of its place in everyday life as a source for information about the nation. People read the news in a "mass ceremony" daily, a ceremony in which participants understand that they are doing the same thing that millions of others are doing. "At the same time, the newspaper reader, observing exact replicas of his own paper being consumed by his subway, barbershop, or residential neighbours, is continually reassured that the imagined world is visibly

7. Ulrich, *A Midwife's Tale: The Life of Martha Ballard, Based on Her Diary, 1785–1812.*

8. Susman, *Culture as History: The Transformation of American Society in the Twentieth Century,* 102, 234, 40.

rooted in the everyday life," Anderson argued. Readers connect to each other through the print they read and form an imagined community—imagined, he said, because its members are not visible or known to each other but connected only through their shared use of media.[9]

Such communities, wrote media historian Thomas C. Leonard, do more than simply read the same message ritualistically; members of imagined communities do more than understand words produced for them. Messages are interpreted and shaped as much by the readers as by the producers of news. In his cultural study of the press audience in U.S. history, Leonard found that, when the newspaper was read aloud in public arenas, debate among audience members became part of how the news was interpreted. Leonard suggests that, in addition to the messages and rituals of news reading, public and private debate among readers helped form a sense of community. Readers in history "talked back" to the news and made choices about what and how they internalized it: "The use of news for one's own purpose was well underway among a broad public in the early stages of mass circulation. Taking just what one wants from the news has turned out to be a major activity of the reading public and a great challenge to the journalists on the eve of the twenty-first century."[10]

Because readers of mass media take part in the shaping of the news messages, Horace M. Newcomb suggests dialogic theoretical models for the study of texts and their relationships to society. Dialogic models are based on assumptions that all forms of communication interact with each other, that texts need to be studied together with the cultures in which they are created, and that mass media are significant in the construction of reality.[11] This work attempts to do just that: to study the texts with which farm women engaged as well as to talk to the women themselves to unlock the culture surrounding them and to identify their construction of the reality in which they lived.

The Social Construction of Reality

To discuss constructions of farm women in this way, through media, is to consider them in the context of the theory of the social construction of

9. Anderson, *Imagined Communities: Reflections on the Origin and Spread of Nationalism*, 33–35, 44.

10. Leonard, *News for All: America's Coming of Age with the Press*, xiii, 116.

11. Newcomb, "On the Dialogic Aspects of Mass Communication."

reality. Sociologists Peter L. Berger and Thomas Luckmann in 1967, in *The Social Construction of Reality: A Treatise in the Sociology of Knowledge,* outlined a history of scholarly thought to address the distinction between what is "real" and what is socially constructed within society; they defined reality as "a quality appertaining to phenomena that we recognize as having a being independent of our own volition" and knowledge as "the certainty that phenomena are real and that they possess certain characteristics." They began from an assumption that reality can be construed differently by different people: "The man on the street does not ordinarily trouble himself about what is 'real' to him and about what he 'knows' unless he is stopped short by some sort of problem. He takes his 'reality' and his 'knowledge' for granted. . . . men on the street take quite different 'realities' for granted as between one society or another."[12]

The question was how and why personal realities differed. Drawing on Marxist concepts of ideology—as ideas serving as weapons for social interests—and false consciousness—as thought that is alienated from the real social being of the thinker—Berger and Luckmann located their search for the condition of reality in external stimuli that influence individual reality. "The sociology of knowledge must concern itself with everything that passes for 'knowledge' in society," they wrote. "Commonsense 'knowledge' rather than ideas must be the central focus for the sociology of knowledge. It is precisely this 'knowledge' that constitutes the fabric of meanings without which no society could exist."[13] But where does such commonsense knowledge come from? And how is meaning made from it? Berger and Luckmann suggest that people construct their realities based on their particular interests, habits, and assumptions and that values and perceptions are derived from interaction with larger societal institutions—such as mass media, religion, and government—as well as from within specific, localized individual experiences.

Sociologist Diana Crane stresses recorded culture (mass media) as central to understanding a given culture as a whole.

> Culture today is expressed and negotiated almost entirely through culture as explicit social constructions or products, in other words, through recorded culture, culture that is recorded in either print, film, artifacts,

12. Berger and Luckmann, *The Social Construction of Reality: A Treatise in the Sociology of Knowledge,* 1, 2.

13. Ibid., 14–15.

> or, most recently, electronic media. The new sociologies of culture deal largely with various types of recorded culture such as information, entertainment, science, technology, law, education and art. Without analyzing the content and effects of recorded cultures as well as the factors that affect the content of recorded cultures, we cannot understand the role of culture in modern society.

Crane notes that culture is so embedded in social structures that most do not recognize when structures are social constructions: "the influence of culture is often 'invisible' in realms of social life that are not depicted by the modern worldview as part of culture."[14]

The role of communication in constructing realities has been emphasized by communications scholar James W. Carey, who articulated the ritual view of communication. Carey said that all communication is geared toward the maintenance of society in time, through the representation of shared beliefs in a symbolic production of reality. According to Carey, "reality is brought into existence, is produced, by communication—by, in short, the construction, apprehension and utilization of symbolic forms." To study communication, Carey asserts, is to "examine the actual social process wherein significant symbolic forms are created, apprehended and used."[15] He is one of many scholars who view communication as a culture-making process, whereby reality is created, shared, modified, transformed, and preserved.[16] Mass media audiences, according to this view, participate in the construction and transformation of their own identities and cultures through communicative texts.

The same scholars emphasize that the meaning of messages is variable and negotiated and that receivers of media messages understand them only within the context of their own cultures and experiences. Significant among these scholars is cultural studies researcher Stuart Hall, who identifies three kinds of messages received through mediated communication: dominant, negotiated, and oppositional. Audience members who share the same background and cultural experiences as the producers of a message will understand the intended message and the meaning "encoded" within it by the producers. This is the dominant

14. Crane, "Introduction: The Challenge of the Sociology of Culture to Sociology as a Discipline," 2–3, 11.

15. Carey, *Communication as Culture: Essays on Media and Society*, 25, 30.

16. Ibid., 33, 43.

meaning. Others, however, who do not share the same cultural background and experiences, are not necessarily privy to all the nuances of meaning intended by the producers of the message. These audience members interpret the message and create meaning from it according to their particular values and experiences. Hall calls this a negotiated reading. The third type of reading, an oppositional reading, occurs when audience members have nothing in common with the producers; they do not understand the message. This means that audiences can and do create unintended meanings for some messages.[17] Hall's work emphasizes audiences as active participants in the formation of meaning, which, according to Carey, in turn shapes culture. Hall's work also is an example of a dialogic approach in that it includes the agency of the audience in shaping the meaning of mass media messages and constructing reality.

The work of such scholars stresses the role of media in the formation and transformation of culture. Producers of mass media messages shape those messages according to their own cultural norms, realities, and experiences; audience members who receive those messages interpret them according to their own cultural norms, realities, and experiences. Together, producers and audiences thus engage in the construction of identity, reality, and culture in a process that is not fixed but is responsive to changes in society and institutions. Much everyday communication about culture and institutions—such as religion or government—comes through media, which, through a mediating role, constitute a mitigating wall between an institution "in the news" and the audience.

The mediated nature of mass communication messages, and the fact that these are created by producers with limited resources and specified routines, means, according to sociologist Gaye Tuchman, that "as newsworkers simultaneously invoke and apply norms, they define them." In constructing news, news workers help to make news a "shared social phenomenon," Tuchman wrote in 1978. She added: "in the process of describing an event, news defines and shapes that event, much as news stories construed and constructed in the early period of the women's movement [portrayed activities] as the activities of ridiculous bra burners."[18] People who report the news do so within the context of their own experiences, of course. Reporters and editors, as agents of their own

17. Hall, "Encoding, Decoding."
18. Tuchman, *Making News: A Study in the Construction of Reality*, 183–84.

cultures, report what is directly relevant to them, and shape what they report as a social phenomenon the audience shares.

Because not all groups in society are fairly represented in newsrooms, some groups have little or no voice in the mainstream press and are excluded from, or marginalized in, the dominant society. Such groups must use alternate media forms to exercise that part of citizenship involving a voice in the public arena. Women's history shows that women have constituted such a group. Women began establishing their own media in the nineteenth century to exercise that element of citizenship. The introduction of one suffrage organ in the late nineteenth century, *The Farmer's Wife,* based in Kansas, bears this out. Though that particular publication lasted only until 1892, the title—and some might say the torch—was passed with the introduction of a national magazine, based in St. Paul, Minnesota, with the same title in 1897. While there is no evidence to support the idea that the two publications were related, it's telling that these two works were aimed at farm women in particular, and aimed at giving those women a voice in public affairs. Examining those texts is critical to understanding American farm women.

The Role of Media in Community-Building

The idea of mass media artifacts being the mechanism by which people build community is not a new one; scholars have discussed the idea in several ways and in several applications. However, no one to date has pulled this body of work together and formulated the model by which others can identify the community formed around the nucleus of a media artifact. In part, this can be explained by the nature of the research conducted in this area. On the whole, it is qualitative and/or historical research aimed at uncovering the links between publication and audience, concentrating on the audience and its consumption of news and events within specific frameworks. One set of research aims to recover readership history by examining audiences of specific publications in unique and unexpected ways. The other, more recent set of research focuses on the role of computer-mediated communication in the everyday lives of the people who use it. Together, a pattern emerges that suggests media do play a role in the building of a community, and it suggests that the role media play can be defined.

Historically, the concept of community has referred to a group of people living in close proximity to each other and sharing a government as well as a cultural and historic heritage. In some contexts, the term *community* also has been used to designate any body of individuals within a larger geographic area who consider themselves distinct from the overall group, as in a religious community, a business community, or a scholarly community.

Over time, the idea of community has shifted in response to changing conditions. Benedict Anderson first articulated the concept of the imagined community: one that exists not just as a function of geographic proximity but as a construct of a group of individuals who trust that others who share their readings of media also share the same communal values.[19] As an example, Anderson discusses the ritual of reading the newspaper at the breakfast table; the reader trusts that others in the houses around him are partaking in the same ritual, creating an "imagined" community of readers just like him. At its core, this concept interacts with the ritual view of communication as articulated by Carey and with the concept of the social construction of reality first articulated by Berger and Luckmann.

With these points in mind, we can see that the concept of "community" does not require its traditional geographic foundation but instead may be applied to any collection of individuals who engage in a collective activity that may in fact be constructed through and by media messages. In a real sense, the community is "imagined," as suggested by Anderson, because its individual members rarely see each other but trust that others are part of their community of interest.

This concept has been demonstrated by researchers who seek to understand media audiences. Thomas C. Leonard's work, focusing on earlier audiences still rooted in geographic proximity, nonetheless provides support for the idea that readers engage with news actively and communally. He demonstrates that even the illiterate "readers" of early colonial newspapers, who listened to others read the paper out loud, "talked back" to the text, contributing their thoughts and opinions about the discourse surrounding news and events of the day—sometimes with their fists rather than with their words.[20] David Paul Nord, who is perhaps best known for his research focusing on communities of journalism, brought this idea forward in numerous contexts, the most convincing and relevant to this inquiry being his study of newspaper let-

19. Anderson, *Imagined Communities,* 33–35.
20. Leonard, *News for All,* xiii.

ters to the editor in a town hit by a devastating contagious illness. Nord shows that readers unable to leave their homes, due to quarantine or fear of the disease, took their opinions and communal discourse to the editorial page, using it to provide both a touchstone for those who still lived and a sounding board for community business that could be carried out in its pages.[21] In both of these historic examples, scholars show that readers of early media texts constructed, modified, and transformed their news, even as they used those texts to maintain their communities.

But the concept of the imagined community does not apply only to readers of news; it applies to television viewers as well. The construction of a television audience acknowledges that the instrument reaches a large number of viewers, who collectively must trust that they are part of a larger communal group engaged with viewing the same programs. While early studies of television focused on the potential effects of its content on public opinion and action, an acknowledgment of the instrument's power to shape community discourse, later studies and theoretical inquiries show that the content aired on television has the power to draw individuals together. Studies of television fandom, for example, pose two questions: What about a particular program draws the interest of the fan? And what compels an individual to become an active member of a fan community?

That fan communities exist cannot be disputed; the body of everyday popular evidence is overwhelming. Henry Jenkins, in the first significant work on this subject, uses as a case study the community of fans surrounding the television show *Star Trek*. He identifies several actions by fans that indicate the existence of an imagined community of the sort articulated by Anderson and others. The primary indicator that individuals considered themselves part of that imagined community is the signifier of a name: Trekkies. Trekkies are those who are fans of the original *Star Trek* series and identify themselves in that way. They also engage in activities that set them apart from the average television viewer: they write fan fiction stories, create folk art surrounding their favorite scenes and characters, and engage in other creative activities, such as the writing of music, that interact with the texts as presented on the original program.[22] These fan activities are acknowledged by other scholars interested in the phenomena of fan community. Lisa A. Lewis,

21. Nord, *Communities of Journalism.*
22. Jenkins, *Textual Poachers.*

Janice Radway, Camille Bacon-Smith, and others have noted that fans engage with texts in ways that could be perceived as parasocial. But in fact, it appears that the texts provide fans with an opportunity to gratify a need for social interaction in eras where geographic community, in its idealized, small-town, traditional form, rarely exists.

With the introduction of computer-mediated communication, individual media users began to use the machine to interact not only as an imagined community but also as a connected group of people discussing their topics of interest in an interpersonal fashion. Media artifacts such as television programs may have provided a basis for the connection, but the community built through the computer-mediated communication network looks much more like the example unearthed by David Nord: in the absence of the ability to see and visit with each other geographically, the medium itself became the tool by which community is maintained.

The model that begins to take shape in understanding the literature and history shows that community may be formed and maintained through the use of a media artifact, whether it be a newspaper, a magazine, or an Internet forum. My research shows that a media artifact can stand as the mechanism by which individuals connect with each other and adds to the growing body of research that demonstrates the means by which that can occur. Farm women, living far from each other in isolated homesteads, were able to connect with each other through magazines that they read and to which they contributed. It appears that a thriving community of farm women used farming magazines to connect with each other, reinforcing commonsense constructions of their lives and values. How they constructed themselves through these media is revealing of their positions socially and politically.

Constructions of Women as Citizens

Citizenship traditionally has been conceptualized as including the rights to vote in elections for public offices and to speak out in public about public affairs. But U.S. women did not fully share these rights before 1920, when the Nineteenth Amendment to the U.S. Constitution gave them the right to vote. In early America, only landowning white men could vote, and only they were presumed to be able to effectively conduct public affairs. Gender norms excluded women's participation in the public arena, and those who attempted to participate were marginalized. Suffrage thus became crucial for women to gain the rights of citizenship—meaning a vote and a voice in public affairs—that men took for granted.

One of the first women to note that women deserved the same citizenship rights as men was Abigail Adams, wife to one U.S. president and mother to another. In correspondence with her husband, John, during the period when he was working as a representative to the first and second Continental Congresses, she reminded him to think of women citizens as he and his fellow representatives wrestled with the construction of their own government. For the purposes of this work, it's worth noting that Mrs. Adams ran the family farm in Massachusetts single-handedly, during a war, while Mr. Adams worked on behalf of his country. This remarkable woman was ahead of her time, however. As a practical matter, the first public acts to bring attention to women's right to citizenship and suffrage seem to date to the 1848 "Declaration of Sentiments and Resolutions," produced by a group of women who gathered that year at Seneca Falls, New York, to discuss women's rights. These women, many of whom had worked for such social causes as abolition, began to identify suffrage as a means to gain participation in public life. Citizenship to them seems to have meant exercising a voice in public affairs, at the very least. But it also meant a civic responsibility to participate in governmental and social actions through the vote. The women's list of grievances began with the denial of suffrage:

> The history of mankind is a history of repeated injuries and usurpations on the part of man toward woman, having in direct object the establishment of an absolute tyranny over her. To prove this, let facts be submitted to a candid world.
>
> He has never permitted her to exercise her inalienable right to the elective franchise.
>
> He has compelled her to submit to laws, in the formation of which she had no voice.
>
> He has withheld from her rights which are given to the most ignorant and degraded men—both natives and foreigners.
>
> Having deprived her of this first right of a citizen, the elective franchise, thereby leaving her without representation in the halls of legislation, he has oppressed her on all sides.
>
> He has made her, if married, in the eye of the law, civilly dead.[23]

23. "Declaration of Sentiments and Resolutions," 139–40.

This passage stressing denial of citizenship to women signaled the beginning of the subsequent, almost unrelenting, seventy-two-year fight for suffrage that would permit women to exercise their rights as citizens.

Literature about women as citizens generally specifies or implies the right to exercise a public voice that could give rise to social change through politics. Media historian Janet M. Cramer identified four images of women in three women's periodicals between 1894 and 1909, a period during which women sought suffrage: woman as mother; woman as morally superior to man; woman as altruistic; and woman as equal to man. These images, which she found predominantly in the *Courant,* an organ of the Midwest Chapter of the General Federation of Women's Clubs—whose members were likely white, upper-middle-class women—were not necessarily linked to citizenship, however. Cramer identified a conflict within the text suggesting that these women, while they believed in civic responsibility, struggled with suffrage as "unseemly" for their stations in life. Women were viewed in terms of class in *Socialist Woman,* an organ for the Socialist Party; the working-class women expressing views in this publication wrote less about civic responsibility than about equality for workers, Cramer concluded. The categories of woman as citizen were barely visible in *Woman's Era,* an African American publication, but Cramer found that "womanhood" was tied to the notion of citizenship in that publication, nevertheless.[24]

Historian Alice Kessler-Harris, in writing about women's labor history in the twentieth century, treated suffrage as relatively minor in a definition of citizenship. She emphasized economic freedom, or the access to financial means allowing independent participation in the polity, as essential for citizen participation:

> The concept of economic citizenship demarcates women's efforts to participate in public life and to achieve respect as women (sometimes as mothers and family members) from the efforts of men and women to occupy equitable relationships to corporate and government services. Access to economic citizenship begins with self-support, generally through the ability to work at the occupation of one's choice, and it does not end there. Rather, it requires customary and legal acknowledgment of personhood, with all that implies for expectations, training, access to and distribution of resources, and opportunity in the marketplace.[25]

24. Cramer, "Woman as Citizen: Race, Class, and the Discourse of Women's Citizenship, 1894–1909," 15–17.

25. Kessler-Harris, *In Pursuit of Equity,* 12–13.

Kessler-Harris suggests that women continued to be systematically excluded from economic citizenship in the twentieth century through legislation that affected nonfarm labor. Further, she asserts, these exclusions rested on deeply embedded social and cultural notions of women as dependent, reliant on familial support, and more interested in the social than the economic impact of the workplace.[26] How these notions affected farm women remains unclear, and even Kessler-Harris recognizes the lack of attention paid to farm women as working women.

In 1929, Emily Newell Blair, president of the Women's National Democratic Club and a former chair of the Democratic National Committee, discussed women as citizens in the context of women's participation in political parties. For a woman newly granted the vote, becoming a party member was a simple affair of identifying herself as Republican or Democrat, but to truly participate in party politics required active involvement in committee work through the party system. Blair said that recruiting such women had been difficult. Women, she said, had not become a political bloc through gaining suffrage. Those who participated in party politics were surrounded by men, with whom they had to form alliances to make progress, and women as a group were still deeply divided along party lines.[27] Blair wrote:

> When it comes to the amount of power given women in political party organizations, one must grant that comparatively little is given them. But then, little responsibility is given anyone in political parties. Members of the party take responsibility and women have been backward about taking it. Their habit is to sit back and then complain because it is not offered them. But once more there is opportunity to take it, if they will.[28]

Blair emphasized in 1929 (nine years after women gained the vote) that women had the opportunity to enter public life as citizens and politicians through participation in political parties; but, she stressed, they had to seize that opportunity.[29]

In 1947, twenty-seven years after gaining the vote, Kathryn H. Stone—a political scientist who was serving at the time as the first vice

26. This argument is the central theme of Kessler-Harris's book and is probably best articulated through the case study she provides in her epilogue; ibid., 290–96.

27. Emily Newell Blair, "Women in the Political Parties," 221–22.

28. Ibid., 224.

29. Ibid., 229.

president of the League of Women Voters—said that women had successfully adapted to their roles as citizens. Woman suffrage had brought a "fresh perspective" and a "fresh interest" in government, both of which benefited all citizens of the United States in their attention to civics, history, and the physical environment. Legitimizing a place for women in the polity benefited all of society because both sexes had become more concerned about "society as a whole." Stone wrote, "This means merely that both men and women are becoming politically more mature."[30] Stone objected to emphasis on women as citizens, as if some special difference affected women's citizenship, because it ignored or obscured citizenship issues everyone shared:

> It is time we stopped talking about "women as citizens," and talked about citizens. The differences between men and women citizens are not great, and those differences which do exist have largely cultural causes which are changing. It would be much to the benefit of our Nation and the world if we could have an end to the analysis of sex differences in citizenship, and use our energy to find ways to meet the difficulties and discouragements common to all citizens in the atomic age.[31]

Stone was most concerned about the cultural differences, particularly between women who were wage earners and those who were not. Women who worked outside the home had, effectively, two jobs; therefore, conducting the work of the third—engagement in civil affairs—would be difficult, if not impossible, for female workers. "Only the short work week, convenient civic opportunities, and powerful motivation will work to offset the disadvantage of the double job. The civic participation of women wage earners will depend to a considerable extent on the attitude of the husband and on whether he is willing to assume his share of the family work." Finally, Stone said that women needed the support of a culture that expected them to participate in civic life and helped erase their guilt at leaving home responsibilities behind in order to do so. "Civic action must become the *right thing* to do."[32]

30. Stone, "Women as Citizens," 79, 80.
31. Ibid., 79.
32. Ibid., 85 (emphasis added).

Farm Women as Political Actors

What's striking about the literature reviewed here is that it implies a lack of women's involvement as active citizens, particularly as civic action is conceived in those sources. Especially indicative of this, the literature assumes a need for political change while, nevertheless, stressing the entrepreneurial characteristics of farm women as a group. But that literature does not generally focus on farm women as political beings. Rather, it generally includes case studies largely rooted in sociology and business scholarship and underexamines the role of women within the farm family. Although scholarship on farm women has been diverse in attention to time period and geographic location, the assumption at the core of much of it is that farm women need to be rallied to facilitate change in their lives and homes. This assumption, inherently ideological, underscores a central component of the kind of scholarship that treats the Lange image, reproduced in the introduction, as symbolizing the lives of all American farm women. From this perspective, farm women need to be prompted by something external to themselves to act politically for change—to engage in civic action as citizen-participants, in other words.

This conceptualization may be due to literature that has documented the conditions under which women in some rural societies exist as inadequate for sustaining political citizenship or, indeed, economic survival. Joan M. Jensen and Anne B. W. Effland, in their introduction to a volume of the journal *Frontiers* devoted to rural women's history, outline a history of scholarship regarding rural women that started in the early 1980s, when a U.S. farm crisis was at its peak. At that point, scholars were first interested in showing that women worked on farms in capacities that included both household production and outdoor farmwork. In the ensuing decade, scholars concentrated on the value of women's roles on farms in different times and places during the last two centuries. That scholarship points up the diversity of settings and family situations that characterizes rural women's lives, showing that generalizations about their lives are futile and misleading.[33]

In recent years, scholars have examined the situations of contemporary rural women in many different countries, seeking commonalities.

33. Jensen and W. Effland, "Introduction," iii, ix–x.

Liv Toril Pettersen and Hilde Solbakken suggested, as late as 1998, that farm women need to be empowered to effect political change. Noting that women's positions on farms in Western industrialized countries remain unequal to those of men, they said women are underrepresented in farming organizations, participate less than men in shaping agricultural policy, and remain undervalued for their roles on the farms. Further, Pettersen and Solbakken say problems persist in efforts to politicize and organize farm women to emancipate themselves from such constraints. Because of the diversity among rural women, a common platform for reform and grassroots organization hardly exists, the authors asserted.[34]

A focus on what an outsider perceives as a need for change in the lives of farm women overlooks the farm women's point of view. And efforts to find strategies for change among farm women that neglect whether farm women themselves see change as needed are likely doomed to failure, some scholars have argued. That is, efforts toward political change imposed by an outside source don't necessarily work; such efforts, to be effective, must come from within the group. Helene Oldrup says farm women have the power to change their own lives. In her work with contemporary Danish women who live on farms, Oldrup points out that most Danish women who marry a farmer today are educated and continue to work outside farming after marriage. And many of those women are not from farm families.[35]

Indeed, Oldrup suggests that the identity of Danish farm women is undergoing change. After interviewing Danish farm women, Oldrup concluded that they tend to distance themselves from the traditional, feminized view of "farm woman," which is associated with work in the household and around the farm. The paid employment pursued by the Danish farm women off the farm remains important in their construction of their own identities. These farm women are "active and knowledgeable actors" in shaping their own lives, identities, and discourse, not only on a personal level but also through their social interaction with other women, according to Oldrup.[36] There may be no reason,

34. Pettersen and Solbakken, "Empowerment as a Strategy for Change for Farm Women in Western Industrialized Countries," 318, 327.

35. Oldrup, "Women Working off the Farm: Reconstruction Gender Identity in Danish Agriculture," 343.

36. Ibid., 353, 356.

therefore, to assume that farm women do not act politically when they believe such action is necessary.

Margaret Grace and June Lennie, after studying rural women in Australia, noted the diversity characterizing that population and that some women shared in common only that they live in rural areas. Grace and Lennie say that, despite those differences, the women's activities and identities do have some similarities. Identity for these women involves four key issues, the authors say: a struggle between affirming traditional identities indicative of the patriarchal rural culture and the desire to take leadership roles in that culture; "the tendency to underestimate the real diversity among women in rural and remote parts of Australia by equating 'rural women' with farming women"; a struggle to identify with different constructions of rural women, including constructions in some scholarship of the women as victims and constructions in mass media of them as heroines; and the rejection of the label *feminist* by many rural women who are trying to effect change. This last point is highlighted with a salient finding: the Australian women who also worked outside the farm were more likely to accept a label of *feminist* than were the women who did not. And while some Australian farm women found association with feminism and its ideals empowering, others said that action was more important than labels.[37]

A question underlying scholarship about the need for political change on the part of farm women seems to be why farm women are not more active in political movements that could significantly—and positively—affect their social positions and their business opportunities. Are farm women politically active without prompting from external sources? Under what conditions are farm women politically active? These questions may divert attention from more important ones. For example, how have farm women constructed their own identities as political beings and citizens? Answering that question may help to answer the broader questions that seem to underlie much literature.

Some scholarship about farm women suggests their central importance in effecting political change. But that scholarship focuses on women's involvement in the business of farming, a source of some farm women's activism. Among those who address this issue is labor scholar Sarah Whatmore, who studied the Marxist concept of petty commodity

37. Grace and Lennie, "Constructing and Reconstructing Rural Women in Australia: The Politics of Change, Diversity and Identity," 351, 352, 361.

production. In her work on the restructuring of British family farms in the 1980s, Whatmore highlights the concept of commodity production as contradicting a tendency toward the separation of capital and labor. She calls the concept central to understanding the family farm, where work is organized around a gender division of labor "structured by the patriarchal institution of the conjugal household and a gender division of property rights structured by patrilineal kinship practices." Her study also shows how women on farms become marginalized "from key positions in regimes centred on family labour to peripheral positions within regimes centred on family property." She concludes, "Gender emerges as a deep-seated feature of the product process itself."[38]

Yet some studies suggest that women hold the greatest power in farming and rural communities. In her study of European peasant communities, Susan Rogers found this to be the case. Men and women behave publicly as if men are dominant, but their dominance operates as a myth, she says. Balance is maintained within communities between the informal power of the women and the overt power of the men.[39] While her study was limited to European peasant communities of the 1970s, Rogers's model also could explain the paradox of American farm women, who are constructed in *The Farmer's Wife* as entrepreneurial, with a sharp business sense. That this construction might be tied to family structures is implied by Sally Shortall, who in her study of Irish farm women suggested that power structures are affected by the process of passing the land down in families. Shortall identifies the neglect of interpersonal relations as a problem in scholarship about farm women:

> The farm-family business is not only a relationship between the farm family and the farm business. It also embodies a whole set of relationships within the farm family. In many ways an understanding of the position of women in farming is often complicated by the discourse of the "family farm." It focuses attention on the family unit rather than the inter-personal, economic and social status positions of those within the family.[40]

Shortall also argues that, to understand the role of farm women, scholars must understand the power structures in farming. Such power structures include "a body of customs, beliefs and social practices that

38. Whatmore, *Farming Women: Gender, Work, and Family Enterprise,* 141, 143, 144.

39. Rogers, "Female Forms of Power and the Myth of Male Dominance: A Model of Female-Male Interaction in Peasant Society."

40. Shortall, *Women and Farming: Property and Power,* 1.

are accepted without question," the most obvious of which is the passing of the family farm to the oldest son. Power also lies in control of resources, especially the property that is farmed. Among the families Shortall studied, the norms tended to exclude women's access to—or at least to marginalize them from—power.

Shortall's overall assumption is the need for change in the lives of Irish farm women, whom she defines as those who began farm life following their marriage to men who owned land and were already farming.[41] Her conclusions are based on the study of Irish farm women's organizations and farm women's educational institutions and on interviews with Irish farm women on their farms. She found that most women enter farmwork through marriage, and their work roles are difficult to delineate because it is impossible to separate women's productive and reproductive work spaces. She found also that few of the Irish women she studied participated in farming organizations, and few had formally studied agriculture. Finally, Shortall concluded that media represent farming as overwhelmingly a male occupation.[42]

But what about American farm women? How have they addressed such issues of power? The family structure is just as important for them, as John Mack Faragher has noted in his study of American farm women of the late nineteenth century. The farm family and household operated as a basic unit of labor; production of material necessities and the reproduction of life itself were not treated as distinct forms of activity but were part of the same process, the self-support of the family. He also argued that both sexes were involved in important portions of the family division of labor; women in particular played central roles in production and child-rearing. Rates of fertility were higher than in simpler foraging and more complex industrial societies; the husband ruled as head of the household, legitimized by a sexually segregated public world and a male state structure. In addition, Faragher identified kinship networks of women as significant to combating social isolation and maintaining a strong and important female cultural tradition.[43]

Membership in rural women's clubs and labor organizations also seems key to the exercise of farm women's power, as suggested by labor scholar Bonnie O. Tanner. She linked farm women's work and entrepreneurial

41. Ibid., 2, 6.

42. Ibid., 142–44.

43. Faragher, "History from the Inside-Out: Writing the History of Women in Rural America."

characteristics through study of American farm women who belong to agricultural women's organizations, including American National Cattle Women, Associated Milk Producers, and Women Involved in Farm Economics. She concluded that women on farms could be described as entrepreneurs—but not because of participation in farming organizations: "Farm women in particular have been largely ignored by historians possibly because plowing a field, slopping hogs, churning butter, making soap, emptying chamber pots, and washing work clothes were not looked upon as great achievements. These tiresome chores, however, kept many a farm business from going under." In particular, when comparing farm women who responded to her survey to their urban counterparts, Tanner found that farm women were more likely to be employed, were slightly better educated, and were more involved in community organizations and in the management and operation of the farm. She also found farm women more likely than nonfarm women to have been elected to positions in their local governments. "The respondents in this study dispel the myth of 'the poor isolated rural/farm woman,'" Tanner wrote.[44]

Research reviewed suggests that many farm women, in the capacity of business partners, kept the farm's financial accounts and were as adept at running the farm as they were at running the farm home. Did mass media represent them in such roles? Given scholarship about the role of media in society, what is known about mass media and farmers—and about mass media and farm women? Scholarship also suggests that farm women maintained a strong cultural tradition through their interaction with networks of other women, including extended family. What role might mass media have played in maintaining such networks?

Randall Weller's mother, and other women like her, did use mass media to connect with each other. They talked about a wide variety of issues in the pages of the magazines they read, and they talked to each other through the farm and rural women's organizations that connected them locally. They were active, engaged women, busy with the running of the home, but also concerned with everyday survival through an economically challenging period in U.S. history. For most of these women, their work and everyday struggles seemed insignificant. But they formed the backbone of much of American culture through the twentieth century, and their struggles—and their influence on the children they raised—should not be underestimated.

44. Tanner, *The Entrepreneurial Characteristics of Farm Women,* 42, 86–87.

2

Farming and the Mass Media

As I talked to women who lived on farms between 1910 and 1960, a common theme arose: reading, and the mass media, were critical not only to the education of the youth on those farms but also to keeping the family abreast of the world outside the farmhouse door. This was particularly important for farms owned and operated as businesses by the people who lived in the farmhouse. How else could the business be maintained? Farmers needed to understand the business conditions, the weather, the pricing of crops, and the political movements in Washington, D.C. More often than not, such reading occurred before bedtime, as the woman of the house read aloud to the family from the papers. It was she, too, who contributed regular advice and small features to farming publications and found thrifty uses for the old newspapers and magazines. Helen Williams's story is typical:

> We subscribed to the Fort Worth Star Telegram. Mother would get dress ideas from newspaper ads, Sears Roebuck catalogs, or Montgomery Ward catalogs. She would use the newspaper to make our dress patterns . . . . Mother would go to the library. She read lots of books to Charles and me. When the Graham Library didn't have the information Mother needed she would write the state library in Austin and have them send her books.[1]

The centrality of media, and their necessity, came through strongly in talks and correspondence with women who lived on farms during this period. Media provided a link to the world off the farm, a potential source of income, and goods that could be recycled for myriad uses on the farm. But the real importance of media in the lives of farmers—both men and women—lay in their ability to maintain the political power of the farming community.

1. Helen Williams to author, June 12, 2007.

Mass Media and American Farmers

In 1949, as research was developing in the burgeoning field of mass communication, political scientist Avery Leiserson wrote that the political power of farmers, and the farm vote, could not be explained solely by economic interest. He named several factors that went into the formation of farmers' opinions on public affairs, including national voting trends, party tradition, nationality, religious issues, personalities in specific campaigns, income, ownership, and wage status. He said a recent trend in opinion and attitude research, called "communication research," had begun to focus on the channels of mass communication and education, "emphasizing the effects of the content and control over these influences upon the attitudes of selected audiences." "But communications research has slighted the farmer as yet. Practically no attention has been directed to influences of mass media upon the rural population as a group."[2]

The oversight that Leiserson noted in 1949 continues today. Scholars have debated the role of mass communication in society from the field's beginning. More recently, attention has turned to the role of mass communication in the formation of identity—of individuals and of nations. But scholars have given little attention to the role of mass communication in farm culture and even less to its role in the formation of farmers' identities. Less research still has focused on farm women.

Farm magazines have been studied to address issues other than the roles of farm women. For example, a 1960 political science dissertation by Norman Franklin Reber focused on farmers' political leanings through a content analysis of material in selected farm magazines that included *California Farmer, Capper's Farmer, Farm Journal, Farmer-Stockman, New England Homestead, Ohio Farmer, Progressive Farmer,* and *Wallace's Farmer and Iowa Homestead.* Reber supplemented study of the 1951 and 1958 issues of these publications with interviews and correspondence with their editors. Reber found that, despite the dwindling rural population, farmers' opinions on public questions continued to be a powerful political force during the 1950s. Stressing that the farm family's media contact came largely through farm magazines, Reber said it was logical to look there for editorial content that might influence the political thinking of farmers. Reber found that agricultural information dominated content,

2. Leiserson, "Opinion Research and the Political Process: Farm Policy as an Example," 35.

with opinion editorials ranking second in space allocated. Entertainment occupied the least space. Among the magazines, Reber found that perceptible differences existed between *Farm Journal* and *Progressive Farmer* and the other magazines he studied. Both *Farm Journal* and *Progressive Farmer* had more entertainment than opinion content—and more opinion and entertainment content altogether than other publications he studied. These two magazines, along with *Capper's Farmer* and *Ohio Farmer,* also had more household how-to articles than farming how-to articles.[3] The *Farm Journal*'s focus on household information suggests that women, the principal household managers, were considered a primary audience for this national magazine.

K. W. Cash noted in a 1927 thesis that more than six hundred agricultural publications existed at that time.[4] According to Cash, it appeared that every agricultural state had at least one farm publication, and three national publications also existed: *Farm Journal, The Farmer,* and *Country Gentleman.* Until its sale in 1939 to *Farm Journal, The Farmer's Wife* also had a national audience; upon its sale, it became an independent section of *Farm Journal,* again for a national audience. In addition, between 1911 and 1926, Curtis Publishing Company sought a rural audience for its national magazines, *Saturday Evening Post, Ladies' Home Journal,* and the aforementioned *Country Gentleman.*[5]

Such media attention to the farm household as an audience had a long tradition by the 1950s, the decade Reber studied. In 1916, the *Bulletin of the Home Economic Association* published the proceedings of the Committee of 50 on Journalism, a round-table discussion that brought together editors of varied magazines and newspapers aimed at women.[6] Participants included Edward Bok, the editor of *Ladies' Home Journal,* and Leonarda Goss, the editor of *The Farmer's Wife.* Goss wrote that her magazine needed to be both practical and inspirational:

> This means that I must know the women it reaches—know their needs and their ideals. I can be no desk editor sitting complacently in my office with the fixed idea that I know "what women want." I must spend much

3. Reber, "Main Factors that Influence the Editorial Content of Farm Magazines," 91, 99.

4. Cash, "The Relationship between Rural Prosperity and Circulation and Advertising in Farm Magazines."

5. Douglas B. Ward, "Barbarians, Farmers, and Consumers: Curtis Publishing Company and the Search for Rural America, 1910–1930."

6. "The Committee of 50 on Journalism."

> of my time among the actual readers of *The Farmers Wife*, studying them, watching their reactions, their modes of expression and response. I dare not be static, for they are kinetic and changing. In other words, I must, in both a literal and a figurative sense, keep close to the soil and at the same time see the hills and sky. Unless I do both these things I shall be creating a magazine for farm women as fiction and tradition have represented them; as my memory pictures them, when years ago I lived on the farm—in short as I think they should be rather than as they are.[7]

Goss recognized that her audience was continually changing, continually responsive to farming and social conditions, and continually in need of content that would help farm women meet their varied needs. Other women editors, later in the period under study, had the same sort of approach to their audiences. Laura Lane wrote that when she started work as editor of *Farm Journal* in 1955, "There was a sharp division between writing about agriculture and writing about the concerns of the farm wife. But these distinctions blurred as I began to write articles encouraging farm wives to be business partners of their husbands."[8]

At the same time, farm women's content was in danger of being dropped altogether. Roy Reiman, chairman and CEO of Reiman Publications, recalls that he was shocked when he discovered in 1970 that *Farm Journal* and *Successful Farming* were dropping their women's sections. The reason given, he said, was that the magazines could not compete with *Woman's Day* and *Family Circle* for advertising dollars. After much work, Reiman launched a no-advertising magazine he called *Farm Wife News.* This later became *Country Woman,* and its success, based on subscriptions only, encouraged Reiman to launch eight other magazines in the same no-ad format.[9] The editor of *Progressive Farmer,* Jack Odle, recalled that, when his magazine spun off its women's content in 1966 into a new magazine called *Southern Living,* the idea was to take the content to urban subscribers with rural roots—the people who had left farms to seek opportunities in the cities.[10]

Claude Gifford, a former *Farm Journal* staffer, said also that editors made it a point to sit down with readers twice a year:

7. Leonarda Goss, "Planning My Magazine," 86.

8. Lane, "A Pioneer Who Didn't Feel Like One," in *Farm Magazines, Milestones, and Memories: American Agricultural Editors' Association, 1921–1996,* 15.

9. Reiman, "All That Fun . . . and I Got Paid for It," in ibid., 70–71.

10. Odle, "When Readers Move, Move to Readers," in ibid., 66–67.

> You'd sit down, preferably with the husband and wife at the kitchen table, and page through from front to back to find out what they had read. You'd try to find why they did or didn't read something. . . . You found that frequently the farm wife read something first and marked it for her husband to read. All of us became better writers and editors through those magazine readership interviews. When you sat down to write something, you imagined yourself at that kitchen table.[11]

The centrality of the kitchen table—normally a gendered image—in this description suggests its importance in the farm home and in the culture of farming. It suggests that farm women not only read farming magazines; they likely played a significant role in selecting political and technical content useful in the family farm business. The salience of that image in media coverage of farms also suggests that farming as a business and as a way of life converged through the farm home.

Women's Magazines

Scholars studying farm women's history have used oral history (Jensen), survey research (Tanner, Rosenfeld), and ethnography (Shortall), but it appears that very few to date have used the farm magazine as a primary source of information about a farm woman's life. One exception is anthropologist Jane Adams, who studied *Farm Journal* to discern the hegemonic construction of farm women's femininity throughout the 1950s.[12] Studies of American women's magazines make explicit the link between advertising content in prominent publications and a developing construction of women as primary consumers during the twentieth century. Indeed, this linkage is a primary point of nearly all the literature reviewed about the history of women's magazines during the period under study here.

Helen Damon-Moore documented the history of the *Saturday Evening Post* and *Ladies' Home Journal* from 1880 to 1910. She shows that the publishers of *Saturday Evening Post* made a concerted effort to attract women as an audience during that period: "Women were viewed as the primary consumers in the culture; in order to make it big with a commercial magazine, then, women had to constitute at least some of the magazine's primary audience." Damon-Moore notes that editors of

11. Gifford, "Carroll Streeter—the Best Editor I Ever Met," in ibid., 86.
12. Adams, "The *Farm Journal*'s Discourse of Farm Women's Femininity."

the two magazines, *Ladies' Home Journal* and *Country Gentleman*, published by the same company, Curtis Publishing, agreed on one central theme during this period: "Women should consume, and men should earn to support that consumption."[13]

Mary Ellen Zuckerman, in the one of the few histories of U.S. women's magazines, argues that publishers recognized women as a viable consumer group, a target for advertisers, and that this situation influenced content in the magazines in such a way that gender roles in American society were reflected, constructed, and reinforced in their pages.[14] Nancy A. Walker contends that between 1940 and 1960 women's magazines had multiple roles, as businesses, as advisers to readers, as expressions of editorial philosophy, and as sources of entertainment and information. She also notes, however, that women's magazines have never delivered perfectly "monolithic" messages about women's roles: "Indeed, precisely in the contradictory messages that the magazines frequently conveyed is it possible to see the domestic as a contested and negotiated concept rather than a proscribed and stable one."[15]

Both Walker and Zuckerman document the long-standing high circulation and prominence of what Zuckerman calls the "Big Six" of women's magazines: *Ladies' Home Journal, Good Housekeeping, McCalls, Woman's Home Companion, Delineator,* and *Pictorial Review.* Both also address other women's magazines that rose to prominence or were of significance in the latter half of the twentieth century, including *Vogue, Cosmopolitan, Harper's Bazaar, Mademoiselle, Seventeen, Glamour, Redbook, Better Homes and Gardens,* and *Woman's Day.* Neither takes note of farm women's publications in any period, however.

In the period beyond 1960, and thus beyond the parameters of this work, the audiences for farming periodicals changed, as more and more people moved from farms into cities. The farm magazines had to adjust to the shifts, and content for farm women was spun off into other publications—such as occurred with *Progressive Farmer*'s establishment of *Southern Living*—or eliminated altogether.

13. Damon-Moore, *Magazines for the Millions: Gender and Commerce in the "Ladies' Home Journal" and "Saturday Evening Post," 1880–1910,* 148–49, 155.

14. Zuckerman, *A History of Popular Women's Magazines in the United States, 1792–1995,* xii.

15. Walker, *Shaping Our Mothers' World: American Women's Magazines.*

Studying Farm Women's Magazines: Method

The fifty-year span from 1910 to 1960 covered in this book thus encompassed radical changes affecting women and farming in the United States. Farmers' political power during this period was significant, as their business underwent technological and social changes brought about by mechanization, war, and population shifts. In the farm home, women read and passed on information over the kitchen table that potentially shaped farm politics. How these women viewed themselves in the role of citizens had implications for the shaping of political power—both for women and for farming—that reached well into the future.

It is important to study constructions of farm women in the media during this fifty-year period because those women contributed to political action originating with farmers and the farm home. And, significantly, farm women during that half-century almost certainly influenced two generations of young people who were raised on farms and moved to cities. Those generations took with them farm women's constructions of citizenship—for men and women—into hotly contested political arenas that arguably shaped U.S. politics and society from the 1960s forward. Learning how farm women constructed citizenship and political action in the fifty years before 1960 may aid in understanding, at least in part, the underpinnings of such U.S. political movements as the perceived ideological shift among the white working class from the left to the right in the 1960s and 1970s. While answering the question of how that shift occurred is not the focus of this work, the research here may supply a piece of that puzzle.

Research for this book identified constructions of the farm woman in selected media and in selected writings by farm women during this fifty-year period in an effort to contribute to knowledge about farm women in American history and culture. Scholars who are interested in farm women encounter problems of limited sources. Few primary sources, such as diaries and letters, have been found, except in cases of farm women known for something other than the locations of their homes and their work. As Jensen pointed out, many prominent suffragists began life on farms and later moved to cities. Laura Ingalls Wilder, the author of the *Little House* series of books, lived and worked on a farm her entire life (a point noted by Rosenfeld). She and her daughter, Rose Wilder Lane, left a substantial archive of material. The daughter's material includes journalistic work and fiction, plus correspondence between the two women.

The questions guiding the research were: How were farm women constructed in selected magazines published between 1910 and 1960? As women? As citizens? As farmers? How were they constructed in farm magazines? How were they constructed in selected "mainstream" women's magazines? What changes are identifiable in the constructions over time—in both kinds of media? How did farm women construct themselves in their own writing during the fifty years? As women? As farmers? As citizens? How did they construct themselves in their letters to the editors of the media studied? How did farm women who were working journalists construct themselves in their writings? What changes are identifiable in women's constructions of farm women over time? What issues dominated the writing of farm women in letters to editors and in their work as journalists? What changes are identifiable in issues dominating women's writing over time? Finally, how do these constructions hold up against the lived experience of farm women during this period, as revealed through personal interviews and correspondence?

The terms *farm* and *rural* appear throughout this work, but they are not interchangeable. A "farm woman" is a woman farmer who is often but not necessarily always partnered with a man in the running of a farming business. A "rural woman" is any woman who lives in a rural area, including those not engaged in the running of a farm business or in the practice of farming. The farming and "mainstream" women's magazines used as sources here addressed both men and women, sometimes as one audience, so the terms *farm* and *rural* are carefully distinguished in reporting evidence from those sources as well. "Mainstream" magazines are defined as magazines that did not specialize in a particular, segmented audience but aimed to appeal to a broad readership. These magazines have general and high circulations.

It was assumed that farm women would be constructed differently in farm magazines, in "mainstream" magazines, and in farm women's writing. Because the social construction of reality is theorized to depend on culture, one might expect a particular dominant construction to be the same—or very similar—across differing sources in the same society at the same time (including institutions such as education, religion, and family as well as cultural artifacts and products such as the media). Constructions are embedded (or anchored) in culture and in people's experiences; as implied earlier and as articulated by Hall, constructions arise through negotiation of meanings. However, realities are multiple, are constantly changing, and are open to being contested. David Domke, for example, found that language used to construct "race" in late-nineteenth-century American newspapers, particularly regarding a construction of African Americans as socially and biologically inferior to whites, was similar within the personal papers, correspondence, and published writings of five different journalists with different backgrounds and platforms. However, Domke's research shows the contested nature of language in the social construction of reality by suggesting that the actual constructions of race differed depending on the journalists' backgrounds. The three white journalists studied—Whitelaw Reid, Henry Watterson, and Henry Grady—used Social Darwinist language in ways that encouraged "attitudes of white superiority" and "abetted a growing indifference among whites toward the concerns of African Americans," while the two African American journalists—Frederick Douglass and T. Thomas Fortune—used that language in ways that "discouraged blacks from believing in racial equality" and "reinforced intensifying racial divisions."[16] Within the microcosm of the nineteenth-century reality studied, race relations were discussed in similar ways, but to different ends.

The three farm magazines studied for this book—*The Farmer's Wife, Farm Journal,* and *Country Gentleman*—were aimed at a farm audience, which included women. Although it is assumed that farm women read all of these, only *The Farmer's Wife* during this period directly addressed farm women; it ran from 1897 to 1970 and was bound into the *Farm Journal* from 1939 to 1970. That combination made the top-ten list for paid-circulation magazines in 1940. *Farm Journal* ran continuously through the fifty-year period studied, but it underwent some format and content changes. *Country Gentleman,* purchased by Curtis Publishing at the beginning of this fifty-year period, had significant circulation increases when Curtis specifically targeted a rural audience, but it folded in 1955; under a new title, *Better Living,* it merged with *Farm Journal* in August 1955. A magazine-type supplement, *Country Gentlewoman,* seems to have evolved out of household content published in *Country Gentleman;* bound into the back of that magazine beginning in the 1930s, that supplement also was included in the research for this book.

The three mainstream magazines studied—*Ladies' Home Journal, Good Housekeeping,* and *Saturday Evening Post*—were aimed at a larger audience of both urban and rural women and men. These were studied to identify constructions of farm women in selected mainstream women's

16. Domke, "Journalists, Framing, and Discourse about Race Relations," 42.

media. The *Saturday Evening Post,* while not technically a farm magazine, addressed a rural audience, and, according to Damon-Moore, its publishers intended to directly address a female audience.[17] (To a degree, it achieved status as a mainstream journal before its demise in the sixties.) It also was on the top-ten list of paid-circulation magazines in 1920 and 1940.[18] *Ladies' Home Journal* was published throughout this fifty-year period, and, while it did not specifically target rural women, it stands out as a mainstream women's magazine among the top-ten paid-circulation magazines in 1900, 1920, and 1940. This point has been noted by other scholars who have used this magazine as a source for understanding changing conditions for women in the twentieth century.[19] *Good Housekeeping,* also a mainstream women's magazine, addressed more practical homemaking issues and may have reached rural women as an audience. It also was one of the top-ten paid-circulation magazines in 1940.

Constructions were identified through close reading of the texts, employing contextualism as a historical methodology. Robert F. Berkhofer Jr. wrote that in approaching historical research, the dominant paradigm is one in which historians look to the past, gather evidence from which to derive "facts," synthesize the material gathered, and discuss it as history. Crucial to such an approach is the understanding that historians can never truly "know" the past; as Berkhofer points out, no matter how many artifacts survive history, they represent only a tiny portion of "full living past reality." If historians seek to understand the past, they must read and acknowledge the materials they examine within the context of the culture in which they were produced.

> Words and sentences must be read in the context of the document, and the document as part of its community of discourse or of the ideological and in turn demand the context of their cultures and times. Likewise, human activities and institutions are to be understood in relation to the larger network of behavior or social organization and structure of which they are said to be part. Social, political, religious, economic, family, philanthropic, and other institutional practices make sense only when placed in their proper social and cultural contexts.[20]

17. Damon-Moore, *Magazines for the Millions,* 148.

18. All statistics regarding paid-circulation magazines come from Carl Kaestle, *Literacy in the United States: Readers and Reading since 1880,* 262.

19. For examples, see Carolyn Kitch, *The Girl on the Magazine Cover: The Origins of Visual Stereotypes in American Mass Media,* and Nancy A. Walker, "The *Ladies' Home Journal,* 'How America Lives' and the Limits of Cultural Diversity."

20. Robert F. Berkhofer Jr., "Narratives and Historicization," 29, 30, 31.

In this book, such a contextual approach was used to derive constructions of farm women from the magazines' texts. For example, in the October 1935 issue of *Farm Journal* Mary R. Reynolds constructed farm women as business partners, in opposition to city women, reinforcing a positive image of farm women as the "one large group" that stays in touch with the business of their husbands, knowing enough about the men's work to be interested in it and to talk about it with them, understanding it as a business partner would.[21] This positive image feeds an overall dominant construction of farm women as business partners in the running of the farm. Reynolds also points out that city women do not have the same opportunities, contributing to an overall secondary construction of farm women as in opposition to urban women. That this passage was written in 1935, at the height of the Great Depression, suggests that the division between women in urban and rural areas, and the emphasis on the farm business, was heightened by the harsh economic conditions of the era. The fact that this passage was written for an American farming audience during this harsh period also suggests that a concerted effort was made to boost farm optimism and farm women's spirits, perhaps in direct reaction to the flood of people leaving the farms.

All six of the selected magazines contain writing by farm women—including letters to the editor and journalistic content—which was similarly studied for farm women's self-constructions. Such a self-construction is exemplified by this passage, written by Mrs. Arnold Bender, a South Dakotan, in 1960:

> Here's my definition of a farmer's wife—namely, me. Wife, companion, pianist, praiser, audience, correspondent, mother, nurse, baby sitter, veterinarian, entertainer, nudger, philosopher, disciplinarian, go-between, advisor on birds and bees, teacher, preacher, tutor sympathizer, planner, budgeteer, banker, laundress, scrub woman, hired girl, dishwasher, seamstress, mender, dietitian, candy dispenser, cook, gift wrapper, egg gatherer, poultry culler, paperhanger, carpenter, painter, plumber, gardener florist, lawnmower, shopper, barber, beautician, hostess, secretary, mechanic, chauffeur, hunter, shoe-shiner, alarm clock, dictionary, photographer, Emily Post, Dorothy Dix, Easter Bunny, Santa Claus, Johnny-on-the-spot, neighbor's left hand, husband's right hand, assistant to the dog when livestock gets out. It does feel good to be important![22]

21. Mary R. Reynolds, "The Home," *Farm Journal* 59:10 (October 1935): 27.
22. "A Farmer's Wife," *The Farmer's Wife,* April 1960, 91.

Bender clearly defines herself as central to the farm home and the business of farming through her long list of identifiers, which encompasses her roles in her home, her business, and her community.

Self-constructions were studied as well in the journalistic writings of farm women, including Laura Ingalls Wilder, who wrote from 1911 to 1926 for the *Missouri Ruralist,* and Rose Wilder Lane, who wrote for Curtis publications during the same period. Lane, who continued relationships with *Saturday Evening Post* and *Country Gentleman* well into the thirties, also wrote for *Good Housekeeping* in the twenties and for *Woman's Day* from 1937 to 1968. Other farm women writers include several regular columnists identified as farm women through their pseudonyms, as well as other women who wrote in specific sections of a magazine. All such writing, where found, was included in the research for this book. Additionally, more than two hundred women who lived on farms during this period contributed to this research through interviews and correspondence, solicited through calls to retirement centers and community groups in rural Kansas, as well as by a request in *Country Woman* magazine, a contemporary publication reaching a national audience defined as women with interests in country living. The contributors who responded to the *Country Woman* request are spread geographically across the American landscape, including Canada.

For the magazine-focused part of this research, a constructed-year sample was used to select the issues to be read. Issues of each of the magazines were studied at five-year intervals of the period from 1910 to 1960, with the exception of *Country Gentleman,* which ceased publication in 1955. For each magazine, the sample included four issues—one from each season of the year—for each five-year interval. For *Saturday Evening Post,* a weekly magazine, the first four issues of each month in the constructed year were reviewed, for a total of 176 issues. This sampling method resulted in a total of 392 magazine issues to study (see Table 2). Data from the supplement *Country Gentlewoman* were included with the data from *Country Gentleman.* (For a complete list of magazine issues studied, see the Appendix.)

In selecting five-year intervals, salient years during this fifty-year span were targeted: in 1910, women were still seeking suffrage; 1915 was a peak year for World War I, during which farmers' profits soared, as well as the year following the passage of the Smith-Lever Act, which established the Federal State Cooperative Extension Service; in 1920 Congress passed the suffrage amendment and sent it to the states for

Table 2. Number of Issues Studied

Journal	Number of issues (1910–1960)
Country Gentleman	69*
The Farmer's Wife	44
Farm Journal	44
Good Housekeeping	44
Ladies' Home Journal	44
Saturday Evening Post	176**
Total	**421**

**Country Gentleman* started this period as a weekly; the first three weeks of each month in the constructed year sample were read for this analysis. The total is to 1995.

***Saturday Evening Post* ran as a weekly for the entire period. The first four weeks of each month in the constructed year sample were read for this analysis.

ratification; 1925 marked the height of Prohibition, just five years after suffrage was passed, and a period when farm profits had dropped significantly; 1930 saw the beginning of the Great Depression, which arguably had the most impact on farming during the twentieth century; 1935 fell at the height of the New Deal years, during which legislation was enacted to create a national farm program of controlled production;[23] 1940 was the year just before the United States entered World War II, when confidence was beginning to rise; 1945 was the last year of World War II, a period during which women's work outside the home was thrust into the national spotlight because women worked in industries after men were sent overseas to fight; 1950 and 1955 were years of intense cold war politics, when debates about the nature of government, fears about the atomic capabilities of the United States and the Soviet Republic, and the return of women to the home after World War II were among significant issues while a particularly speedy exodus from the farms to the cities occurred; and 1960 brought election of the nation's first Catholic president, helping to bring to the forefront social issues that fueled public debate and controversy throughout the next decade.

Each of these years touches on issues of significance politically and socially to women as well as to farming. The entire issue of each magazine in the sample was studied to gather data to answer the research

23. Allin, "An Instrument of Public Policy," 1100, 1101.

Table 3. Sample Matrix, *Ladies' Home Journal*

	Jan	Feb	Mar	Apr	May	Jun	Jul	Aug	Sep	Oct	Nov	Dec
1910	•			•			•			•		
1915		•			•			•			•	
1920			•			•			•			•
1925	•			•			•			•		
1930		•			•			•			•	
1935			•			•			•			•
1940	•			•			•			•		
1945		•			•			•			•	
1950			•			•			•			•
1955	•			•			•			•		
1960		•			•			•			•	

questions, which sought to determine how farm women were constructed as women, as citizens, and as farmers, and whether those constructions changed over time. These magazines provide scholars with a means for understanding the social construction of these women's realities during these fifty critical years. The magazines themselves provided a touchstone for farm women, an opportunity for reading and sharing news with family, but also for engaging with other women across geographic distances. Each magazine offers insights about what issues were important to farm women as well as about how the women viewed their world. And through the interviews and correspondence with women who lived that experience, this research underscores the centrality of media to the women, whether they read one of the magazines studied here or the John Deere catalog. These cultural artifacts provide us with a long-ignored voice: that of the American farm woman.

3

Farm Women
"The Typification of the Thing America Needs"

"My mother [Pearl Smith Jones] was born May 2, 1891, and died April 6, 1993," wrote Dorothy Jones Kinnard from Pendleton, Indiana.

> She had been married six years when my father died during the flu epidemic in 1919. They had just bought a 160-acre farm on which they lived and had a boy, Earl, age 4, and a boy Carroll, age 2, and me, Wilma, 1 day old. She had just gone to the 8th grade, and was given a choice—piano lessons or high school—and she chose the piano lessons. She was from a family of 11 children on a farm, so she knew nothing else but to stay on the farm.
>
> Back then, there was no help, and the court took over [after her husband died] and put us up for adoption. Only through the heart of the judge in Anderson—he said he was going to give this woman a chance and would personally take responsibility for her—that was the only way she got to keep us. Well, she continued to work harder than any man and every year reported to his office. She raised chickens, milked cows, had sheep, hogs. She would start milking at 3 a.m. and when we got home from school would be milking. We ate what we raised—had no money to buy much—did buy sugar, spices, crackers—baked our bread, ground our flour. We lived on a creek and when we needed something for a meal, she would say, "Go to the creek and bring us a fish." Our grandmother helped me pick the ducks for the feather beds.
>
> We all three graduated from high school, but there was no funds for higher education. When I was 21, I was working in an office in Anderson. Mom and I went to the judge's office and he released her and bragged on her with tears in both their eyes. And for all those years [of supervising] he didn't charge her a cent.
>
> She continued to live on the farm until she was 97, although she stopped driving at 90.[1]

Kinnard's story describes her mother as a woman who, faced with adversity, plunged fiercely into running her own business in order to

1. Dorothy Wilma Jones Kinnard, Pendleton, Indiana, letter to author, July 2, 2007.

keep and raise her three children. Pearl is the kind of woman who was recognized as typifying the American farm woman among the mainstream magazines that talked about them, particularly during the period in which Pearl ran her farm.

Themes in each of the three mainstream magazines catering to women studied here—*Ladies' Home Journal*, *Good Housekeeping* and *Saturday Evening Post*—suggest particular audiences and perspectives. While similar constructions of farm women were found in the magazines' content in the first twenty years of this study—from 1910 to 1930—diverging constructions among the three were seen after 1930. A notable sparsity of coverage of farm women was observed in these three magazines, and this alone suggests a lack of attention to the diversity within the American mainstream culture and a divide between farm and urban cultures. It also implies that the editors of these mainstream magazines either viewed women as one homogenous group or simply ignored the diversity among women.

The magazines' contents revealed several themes. First, farm women were constructed in opposition to urban women; the theme of urban versus rural or farm versus city life permeates much of the content studied. Second, when addressing such issues as women's activism, citizenship, or relationship to civic affairs, magazines addressed women as a whole rather than as a diverse population with varied needs and interests. Third, farm women were constructed as capable businesswomen, particularly within the *Saturday Evening Post*, in which content appeared to chiefly address business interests.

Rural versus Urban Women

Farm women often were seen as having the same interests and needs as their urban counterparts, even as farm life was constructed in opposition to urban life. This dichotomy was particularly apparent in *Ladies' Home Journal*, in which content was regularly directed to both audiences. Life in the city was depicted as one of leisure, recreation, and culture, while life on the farm was depicted as one of labor and restricted leisure activity. Content in both *Ladies' Home Journal* and *Saturday Evening Post* across all fifty years also depicted concern over the exodus of women and men from the farm to the city.

In the May 1915 issue of *Saturday Evening Post*, for example, Herbert Quick used the phrase "The Great Farmer's Strike" to describe the situation in the Middle West of farm children growing up and leaving the farms in droves. The fact that families were leaving the farms for cities, Quick said, was a cause for concern. He cited a recent survey of elementary schoolchildren in Wright County, Iowa, that asked what they intended to do for their life's work—farming or something else? "Eighty-five percent of the boys and almost all of the girls declared that, whatever they might or might not do as life work, they certainly would not do any farming," Quick related, noting that the few exceptions were important. However, two years later, he wrote, the same question asked of the same group of students revealed the inverse—nearly all of the boys and 85 percent of the girls wanted to live and die on the farm.[2]

Quick's article touches on the complicated issue of the rural exodus to the city, situating it among problems with education of country youth and the overall fear with which many city dwellers viewed the shift in population. Would a lack of farmers mean a lack of food? Quick also notes the benefits of country living: economic independence, a steady job outside an office setting that will never go away, and conditions under which "wife and children are economic assets instead of liabilities."[3] In a magazine focused principally on business success, women and children were viewed as assets to the farm business, suggesting they were significant and important in a way that they were not in the city. The fact that both boys and girls were surveyed suggests that the surveyors—and the editor—considered women important to farms. Other articles in *Saturday Evening Post* also reflected growing concern over the farm business and the loss of farm families to the city. Still others enumerated specific progressive farm methods, all framed in the context of Europe's food shortage associated with World War I and fear that a similar shortage could occur in the United States.

The growing divide between city and farm dwellers also is evident in *Ladies' Home Journal* issues from 1910 and 1915. A regular column featured "The Country Contributor," an older farm woman with grandchildren who wrote about contemporary farm conditions and women's roles on farms. Her work contrasts with the rest of the content in the magazine, which highlighted fashion, dressmaking, and the joys of urban living. This contrast, manifest in the language used to identify the column

2. Herbert Quick, "The Great Farmer's Strike," *Saturday Evening Post* 187:45 (May 8, 1915): 3–4.

3. Ibid., 4.

as the words of a "plain country woman," set up a dichotomy between the worlds of the farm woman and the city woman. Life on the farm was hard, but farmwork produced a good, solid, plain living, wrote "The Country Contributor." A kind of nostalgia, colored perhaps by the sense that the world was changing, pervades this woman's column. Farm life is written about as a plain life that is sweet and unfettered by the consumerism making inroads into American culture.

"The Country Contributor" discussed the idea of farm life as plain and idyllic from a commonsense perspective. For example, she wrote in 1910, "My voice comes to you from the kitchen, not from the lecture platform nor the pulpit. I know whereof I speak, and with authority I place joy in labor as the first blessing of poverty after the common blessings of life which we all know are no respecters of money or class." This kitchen authority also backed the idea of women as wage earners outside the home; encouraged making clothes rather than buying them; and supported the idea that women should be paid for their domestic work.

> The Only Real Grievance that Woman Has Against Life is that she is not paid for her service in actual cash. Work for work's sake and service as its own reward are real things and never to be depreciated, but wage is part of the joy of labor, and the wife's wage should be made more tangible to her understanding. How quickly she would outgrow her foolish and pettish passion for finery once she saw herself a recognized worker with her own bank account! As it is, she sees herself in most cases subservient to "him," a bondswoman working for board and clothing, dependent upon "his" generosity for her "spending money."[4]

"The Country Contributor" took issue with women who failed to improve their own circumstances and assert their individual rights. In February 1915, a column by "The Country Contributor" and one by "A Daughter of Today" were placed side by side as if they debated traditional ideals of the country woman versus modern ideas of the young urban woman. However, they addressed women's roles in different ways. The "Daughter of Today" spoke out against the use of the term *old maid* to represent unmarried women, pointing out that times had changed. Women did not need to marry because the alternative was no longer "slavery," she wrote, and unmarried women could and

4. "The Ideas of a Plain Country Woman," *Ladies' Home Journal,* January 1910, 34.

did have value for public life. Moreover, she said, addressing a larger audience of women through her story, society still did not acknowledge the worth of unmarried adult women in public life:

> We don't bring up our daughters today to feel that they must marry at all costs, as they did when there was no life but slavery for a woman outside of marriage. We tell our girls that marriage is the greatest happiness, the noblest service, the truest fulfillment that can come to a woman. We tell them that all their lives should be a preparation, a striving to develop the best that is in them, so that they may be ready for the man who is worthy of that best when he comes—if he comes. But if we are honest and fair-minded, we tell them at the same time that no marriage can be a spiritual or economic compromise and be good; that any marriage which is not a real union of heart and body and mind is unhappy, and that if the right man does not come it is better to go on alone seeking other service and other fulfillment. Some of our best and bravest girls take us at our word; they shut their eyes to money and a home when it is not supported by character, and they do go on alone.
>
> And when they've done it you sneer at them for doing it, instead of helping them along their way, smoothing it and making it less lonely. I say that's mean and cowardly, or if it isn't that, it is five centuries behind the times. You can take your choice.[5]

"The Country Contributor" focused on a different aspect of the problem of women unhappy with housekeeping. Her view, that women who married needed to make the best of the situation in which they found themselves, placed the onus for being happy on women's shoulders; if women did not like their individual situations, they should change them. She wrote of women having choices and suggested that they could choose to be happy:

> We have outgrown the idea that all women should be domesticated, and the newer (and worse) notions that the kitchen is narrowing and that all women should be "liberated" from the "drudgery" that narrows the soul. We have learned a great deal about drudgery, learned that much which we have called drudgery is only so when we do it in a drudging way.[6]

5. "The Ideas of Two Women: A Daughter of Today," *Ladies' Home Journal,* February 1915, 26.

6. "The Ideas of Two Women: A Plain Country Woman," *Ladies' Home Journal,* February 1915, 26.

This argument is complicated, however, by the notion of individual choice. "Anybody can quit if he wants to badly enough. The point is that you do not really wish to quit; you only wish to complain. You wouldn't leave your 'man' for a million dollars. No, you just wish that 'he' would do differently," she wrote, pointing out that it takes two to make a relationship work. "The Country Contributor" added that the lack of standards and values within culture had seriously compromised the decision-making process for young people. "We need set rules and standards—we are suffering intensely just now from the lowering of all our old standards." Yet, in a later editorial debate, "The Country Contributor" conceded that times must change: "there is less chance for [girls of today] to marry. To offset this there is much more chance for business careers for them. It hurts a little, but it is a sentimental notion which we must fling behind us—that woman was made for man's helpmate and that her place is at home—the home which he works to sustain for her."[7] The young urban woman and the older country woman appear to disagree, but at the core they share key values. The idea of choice, and that women have choices that should be supported, remains central in both columns.

A contrast between the "plain" country life and city life also was apparent in the kinds of fashions advocated in *Ladies' Home Journal.* In features that offered patterns for clothing and pictures of what was fashionable, the dress for "country women" was not as highly decorated as the dress for the urban debutante. Patterns called for garments that, while in the fashion of the city, were loose-fitting and unadorned with the extra frills seen on the urban fashions.[8] The attention to the loose cut and lack of adornment for country fashions, perhaps to allow room for freedom of movement to accommodate the kind of work "country women" did, underscores the practicality of dress for country women as opposed to the tight-fitting skirts and yards of ribbon and lace that characterized the urban fashions featured in the magazine. The placement of advertisements in the magazine helped to highlight this contrast. Notions and ribbon were advertised next to fashion illustrations and patterns for the urban woman, while an ad for household detergent appeared next to "The Country Contributor" column in the same month.

7. Ibid.; "The Ideas of Two Women: A Plain Country Woman," *Ladies' Home Journal,* May 1915, 46.

8. "The Country Woman's Clothes: By a Country Woman," *Ladies' Home Journal,* October 15, 1910, 22.

Farm women were described as "wholesome," "plain," "practical," and "straight-laced" in *Ladies' Home Journal.* The language used to discuss farm women set them apart from city women, who were described as fashionable and gregarious. As "The Country Contributor" wrote in November 1915, "The mania for town life has robbed the farms and the country churches of their best people, and though just now a tide of young people, educated in our state institutions, is flowing back to the farms, their life really centers about the town, since automobiles make it easy for them to come and go." She lamented the loss of the "landed aristocracy" of farmers in New England as she paid particular attention to farm women, noting that they were the center of the prosperous farmhouse and happy farm family life.[9]

In another example, Anne E. P. Searing wrote in May 1915, "You farmers cannot run your farms without women any more than you can run them without men, and you are up against the hard fact that women are far less willing to live on farms now than their grandmothers were." She added, "While as for marriage, the most prosperous farmer knows full well that he is accounted far less eligible than the city clerk on a small salary." This succinct summation of the problem for farmers appears in concert with the acknowledgment that women could work just as hard in the city, for a living wage, and have time left over for recreation and culture. "If the girl must cook, wash, iron and bring up a family with her own unaided hands, she prefers to do it in a handy little city flat, where . . . ever necessity is literally within hand's reach," Searing wrote. The picture she paints of farm life for women, one of unceasing work for no pay and no thanks, is not a rosy one; it contrasts sharply with life in the city, which she depicts as a place where recreation and modern conveniences abounded.[10]

In the 1925 issues of *Ladies' Home Journal* read, the contrast between city and farm women was also seen consistently. Farm women were described as plain while city women were described as pretty. Notably, a respect for farm women was seen in an editorial discussion about fireside industries that sprang up on farms all over the country.

Home economic news also included a wide variety of topics of interest to farm women and contributed to the construction of farm women as businesswomen who were central to the operation of the farm business. Yet continued emphasis on pretty clothes and fashions of and for city

9. "A Plain Country Woman," *Ladies' Home Journal,* November 1915, 30.
10. Searing, "What Can I Do on the Farm?" *Ladies' Home Journal,* May 1915, 48.

women leaves an impression that farm women were viewed as out of style and unfeminine, even unintelligent, especially about the important details of fashion. For example, in a January 1925 editorial, Alice Ames Winter discussed several home economics studies, including one that directly contrasted the spending habits of rural and urban girls on clothing. The research showed, she reported, that girls from rural districts "spent more and got less for their money than city girls" and that they also bought more inappropriate and less serviceable garments. These young rural girls and their mothers needed help to find the correct, proper, least costly, and most serviceable clothing, Winter wrote.[11] Farm women's business sense was being measured here by their ability to shop and dress as city women did.

In the *Saturday Evening Post,* concern about the exodus from farms to the city also was seen in 1920, and articles pointed out that food production was increasing. The postwar land boom kept reporter Harry O'Brien traveling in farming states, talking to farmers about the speculative land prices that were tempting many to sell off acreage. The exodus to the cities was spurred in part by land speculators because farmers were tempted by the ready cash, and some succumbed. But O'Brien wrote of one who did not and suggested that farmers' wives had a say in whether the family farm would be sold. His reporting shows that at least some women chose to stay on farms:

> I did not quite realize just what it meant to be offered a big price for a farm until one night I was visiting with an Iowa farm family with whom I am well acquainted. Someone knocked at the door and the man of the family, who owns the farm, went to the door. Two strangers were there. He stepped outside and I heard a murmur of voices for some time. Then the men went away and the farmer returned, smiling.
>
> "Those men just offered me $500 an acre cash for the farm, Mary," he said to his wife. "What about it? Shall we take the $80,000 and let them have it?"
>
> "Well, I should say not!" replied the wife.
>
> "Why should I sell?" the farmer said, turning to me. "I have lived on this farm thirty years all told. I know it from end to end. I have built me this good home here. Here are my friends and relatives. I am near to town and a shipping station. I am a farmer and expect to farm all the rest

11. Winter, "Splendid Government Service if You Ask," *Ladies' Home Journal,* January 1925, 23, 103ff., 23.

of my days. So why in the world should I sell this farm and move away to a strange neighborhood at my time of life?"[12]

As such stories circulated through the *Saturday Evening Post,* other stories in *Good Housekeeping* seemed to directly pit farmers against consumers, with consumers constructed as urban homemakers. Although *Good Housekeeping* steadily addressed women's roles as citizens and as businesswomen throughout the period under study, the magazine did not specifically address farm women per se. In fact, what is most striking about the issues of *Good Housekeeping* studied is the absence of farming interests in general. Farming was rarely mentioned, and farm women hardly at all. This absence of farm women was surprising, given the main themes that characterized the magazine: women's domestic work as important in its own right; women's civic work on behalf of the home as important work; and domestic science as important for keeping a happy home and a safe home. Each of these themes would seem to have been of interest to farm women, and the emphasis on domestic science, with articles from experts about food production, would seem to have been important to farm women's roles as the main producers of farm food products for home consumption and for sale.

Good Housekeeping was an advocate for the consumer during the fifty-year period. Its Good Housekeeping Seal of Approval had been instituted in 1910, and advertisements explained that the seal would be used to show that food and other household products advertised in the magazine had been tested by a staff of domestic scientists and approved for domestic use. *Good Housekeeping* editors solicited help from readers to identify consumer fraud and to share methods of cutting consumer spending. Spending habits of men and women were discussed, and it was clear throughout the journal that the editorial staff assumed women bore the responsibility for household spending.

In the 1910 issues studied, the magazine's focus was on instruction for women in domestic science. Articles told how to keep a good home, contribute to public health, raise children, make things for the home, choose a home, and manage salaries and household budgets. Many articles were written by college professors, including women professors of domestic science at institutions such as Columbia University. The

12. O'Brien, "Frenzied Farm Finance," *Saturday Evening Post* 192:36 (March 6, 1920): 141.

magazine might have been read by its subscribers as if it were a scientific journal that focused exclusively on household and domestic science.

A major article in 1910 dealt with a report on the cost of living, noting several key issues raised: (1) the cost of living had steadily increased in the previous decade; (2) incomes of salaried men showed no proportionate increase; (3) the cost of living was at that time "perilously close to the average income of the middle or salaried class, which includes clerks, bookkeepers and professional men"; (4) this class had the heaviest burden "inasmuch as the laboring class has not an increasingly high standard of living to maintain and therefore feels the pressure less"; (5) a variation in prices for necessities in different regions of the nation was out of proportion to the conditions of the regions; (6) the South had a lower cost of living than the North, due in part to the warmer climate, which meant lower fuel and clothing bills; (7) where "the negro" worked, there was a tendency toward lower wages; and (8) "protected" labor had less to complain about than did members of the middle and salaried professional class.[13]

Prices for commodities, listed in the article, emphasized high costs for farm produce, such as chickens, eggs, and milk—yet the farmer was not mentioned. Still another article, in the April 1910 issue, blamed the high cost of commodities on farmers, who, the author—Eugene Davenport, dean of agriculture at the University of Illinois—said, had exhausted their farms' soil and thus lessened the yields for grain and other staples per acre sowed. Further, in an attempt to get better prices for meat and other produce, farmers had shipped their products to the city via the railroad rather than selling locally, which further raised prices to include the cost of transportation.[14]

The two articles suggest an editorial emphasis on consumer issues as a function of city living and a disconnection between the farming business and cost of living. There was no evidence in the magazine issues read of an understanding of farming as a family business, or of the pricing of commodities as beyond farmers' control.

Good Housekeeping in April 1910 addressed the issue of working women, asking in a survey of five hundred unmarried men whether they could support working women better than the women could support themselves, and whether that was a factor in deciding to marry.[15] The questionnaire,

13. "Where Prices Are Low—and High," *Good Housekeeping* 50:1 (January 1910), 75.
14. Davenport, "Why Food Is Costly," *Good Housekeeping* 50:4 (April 1910): 435–39.
15. "Bachelors—Why?" *Good Housekeeping* 50:4 (April 1910): 461–65.

printed in its entirety, did not include farming as a viable occupation for women, nor did it ask unmarried male farmers their opinions about working women. "Working women" in this article appeared to mean only unmarried women who worked in the city as clerks, teachers, secretaries, or in similar salaried professions. Another survey reported in July 1910 dealt with the spending habits of men and women within a marriage and showed that married women generally held the responsibility for household buying. Indeed, women who responded to the survey were emphatic about their roles as equals in managing the household. "I am treated as an equal partner," wrote a woman from Wisconsin. "I am in full control of household affairs and expenses."[16]

Stories about women's work roles and the management of household expenses suggest that the editors and writers valued women for their brains and abilities. The lack of attention to farm women may mean either that the magazine was more focused on urban living or that farm women were assumed to be a part of the audience and to have the same concerns and needs as city women. Many letters written by women in response to surveys asking about working women and domestic spending came from states that had predominantly agricultural populations during this period, such as Kansas and Wisconsin. This suggests that farm women were likely part of the magazine's audience.

The 1915 issues of *Good Housekeeping* studied contain similar questions about women's roles. A feature article by Nancy Musselman, for example, discussed professional women who seem "sick at heart" over their lack of a home and family, and women with families who, conversely, want the life these professional women supposedly have. Musselman wrote that she believed the industrialization of society, in forcing industry out of women's hands in the home, had also forced a choice upon women—to work "out" (outside the home) or to raise a family. Society had viewed this as "a logical sequence of a larger and inevitable movement toward the socialization of the industries," Musselman wrote, but it was a sequence that entailed the suffering of women. She explained:

> The fact that the old industries have slipped out of her hands, and that she has had need to follow them in order to find social service to do by no means implies that such service will be the death of her equally ancient and inherent impulse toward those personal relationships upon which

16. "The Family Pocketbook," *Good Housekeeping* 51:1 (July 1910): 9–15.

> homes are founded. She has her business, but she wants her child; she has her profession, but she wants her love; she has her office, but she wants her home. And why, if you please, should she not have both—should she not have all—should she not be allowed to live out her life to the fullest, satisfying all the good impulses of which she finds herself possessed?[17]

In placing the impetus for women working in the professions squarely on the industrial revolution, Musselman suggests that a false choice led to urban women's discontent: women on farms still worked in a "home industry"; women in cities were forced to choose between working at home or in a profession. Nevertheless, in 1915, a regular feature about women in the professions targeted young women who were interested in varied careers including medicine, journalism, and law. In 1920, this feature continued to provide career advice, in dentistry, nursing, and politics.

Silence about farm women continued to be evident in issues of *Good Housekeeping* studied from 1925, 1930, and 1935, as the magazine focused more tightly on domestic science and consumerism, health issues, homemaking tips, and domestic articles. An exception was in the writing of Eleanor Roosevelt, who in August 1930, as the first lady of New York State, was asked by the *Good Housekeeping* editor to discuss the job of a wife, addressing the questions "Just what is a wife's job today? In what respect does it differ from the job as it used to be? How is it managed by women who manage it in the modern way?" The questions cast the role of "wife" as a job, to which women are promoted upon their marriage. The questions also suggest that the job description for "wife" had changed by 1930. "I had come to realize that the questions I was asking were too big for a mere man to answer," wrote the interviewer, M. K. Wisehart. Roosevelt's answer was illuminating (if not revealing):

> I think we must all agree that in the wife's job there are three fundamentals—being a partner, being a mother, and being a housekeeper and homemaker. Formerly, if we had been arranging the phases of the job in the order of their importance, I think we would have put being a mother first and next being a housekeeper and homemaker, and then being a partner. But today we understand that everything else depends upon the success of the wife and husband in their personal partnership relation. So from the modern point of view that comes first.

17. Musselman, "The Homesick Woman," *Good Housekeeping* 61:5 (November 1915): 567ff., 570.

> The most successful marriage I have ever known was the most complete in its partnership. . . . Partnership! Companionship! And fitness for it! It is the major requirement for modern marriage. . . . I have never thought it was any more a wife's job to keep her husband's mind off his business worries by entertaining him than it is a husband's job to entertain his wife and keep *her* mind off the thousand and one irksome duties that may be tiring her![18]

Such partnerships, Roosevelt said, include sharing the parenting and homemaking responsibilities and taking a strong interest in each other's work. In addition, women who keep a career outside the home must be prepared to put home first if necessary to sustain the whole of the partnership.

In 1930 and in 1935, farm women also were not mentioned in the issues of *Ladies' Home Journal* read for this study, which seems remarkable when one considers the effect of the Great Depression on farms—and the iconic Lange photograph described in the Introduction. Women's citizenship (discussed below) was still constructed as engagement in social life and affairs, suffrage, and women's issues. In fact, one editorial predicted that, given the progress made by women, the term *feminism* would disappear from the nation's vocabulary.[19] But attention to farm women's issues was not found. The focus of the issues read from the 1930s remained homemaking, domestic science, child rearing, and women's legal issues. Home financing, divorce law, and politics were discussed in articles that implicitly addressed women as one monolithic group, but the topics covered assumed an audience of upper-class urban women. Editorials in these 1935 issues bemoaned raised taxes that went toward government-sponsored relief efforts for the Great Depression. Fashion pages touted the "smart young women's tweeds" for "scholars" at Vassar and Yale.[20] Most noticeable in these magazine issues from the 1930s is the complete absence of farm and rural matters; the absence is particularly striking compared to content studied from the previous twenty years, when farm women and their needs and interests were evident from one issue to the next of those read. It is possible, given the conditions on farms and the depressed U.S. economy in the 1930s, that the editors simply chose to focus on the audience that was most likely

18. "Mrs. Franklin D. Roosevelt Answers a Big Question," *Good Housekeeping* 91:2 (August 1930): 34–35, 166ff.

19. "Ten Years of Suffrage," *Ladies' Home Journal*, August 1930, 22.

20. *Ladies' Home Journal*, September 1935, cover, fashion feature.

to be able to afford a subscription, and thus neglected the rural and farming audience. Even if farm women were treated in issues not read, their absence in those studied is still significant.

In 1940 and in 1945, rural women were again seen in the issues of *Ladies' Home Journal* that were studied. Gladys Taber's "Diary of Domesticity," a monthly column written from her Vermont country home, discussed country life as idyllic in comparison to the poverty and pace of city life. "I like to feel the house snug and quiet and clean around me, firelight on the books, windows blurred with silver," Taber wrote in February 1945. "I really have time to look at my Heritage books with the lovely illustrations, or reread Keats' Letters." Taber's columns often extolled the delights of rural living, even as other features within the magazine discussed its problems.

"What Do the Women of America Think about Discipline in the Home?" was the title of a short item in April 1940. Presenting the results of a recent poll of readers, the author discussed the pros and cons of "whipping" children. Sixty-three percent of readers responded "no" to the idea of punishing children by whipping; however, more farm mothers than city mothers said that whipping was an acceptable punishment. The fact that the results were broken down between city and farm women suggests that the two groups were perceived as exemplifying distinct cultures in the United States.[21]

The contrast between these two cultures was also highlighted in a romantic fiction story, published in *Ladies' Home Journal* in May 1945, titled "The Farmer's Daughter."[22] The story detailed the everyday chores of a farmer's daughter who had become mistress of the farm after the death of her mother. The story suggests that the common sense of the farmer's daughter, Nell, exemplifies plain thinking in a troubled world. Her romantic interest, a city schoolteacher named Thomas, represents that troubled world. However, an undercurrent within the story suggests that Nell, as an uneducated farm girl, really isn't good enough for the city schoolteacher. In the way of romantic fiction, the two end up together, with Thomas realizing that their differences don't matter and with Nell giving into a need to take care of Thomas. With Nell cast as caregiver, Thomas is cast as wage earner, and Nell is asked to leave the farm for the city.

21. "What Do the Women of America Think about Discipline in the Home?" *Ladies' Home Journal,* April 1940, 57.

22. Nelia Gardner White, "The Farmer's Daughter," *Ladies' Home Journal,* May 1945, 17–18, 74ff.

Farm women were mentioned again in *Good Housekeeping* in 1940, this time in a three-part series discussing women in politics written by Eleanor Roosevelt. She reported that the number of women elected to office had peaked and then declined during the twenty years since women had gained the vote. She noted, too, that men still tended to elect a man if a man was running, and that women who ran for office often lost simply because they ran against a man. Those women who did hold public office were extraordinary, hard-working women who treated politics as a serious year-round business—in contrast to many male politicians who treated their jobs as seasonal games. "There are moments when I think that women's fervor to work continuously does not make them very popular with the gentlemen!" Roosevelt wrote.[23]

Later in the series, she touched on farm women's roles when she argued that women must not only unite, they must also somehow convince men to look beyond that unity to the individual women they are. Women represent varied interests and levels of ability that should not be obscured by defining all women by their sex, she argued.

> The farmer's wife, for instance, must get into her day more work than does the average businessman. Many a woman runs the family home on a slender pay envelope by planning her budget and doing her buying along lines that would make many a failing business succeed.
>
> It will always take all kinds of women to make up a world, and only now and then will they unite their interests. When they do, I think it is safe to say that something historically important will happen.[24]

This recognition of women's diversity addresses farm women as individuals with unique needs that do not always correspond to the needs and interests of women in the city. This line of discussion continued in the same issue through a fashion article that touted a seven-piece wardrobe for the country for under forty-five dollars. Accompanying pictures showed an attractive model in varied poses, the most unbelievable of which had her wearing a skirt and holding a pitchfork while standing on top of a haystack.[25] (It seems that recognition of farm women as women with interests and needs different from those of city women did not include a realistic notion of what farm women's lives were like.)

23. Roosevelt, "Women in Politics," *Good Housekeeping* 110:1 (January 1940): 18–19, 150.

24. Roosevelt, "Women in Politics," *Good Housekeeping* 110:4 (April 1940): 45, 201–3.

25. "Seven Piece Country Wardrobe for About $45," *Good Housekeeping* 110:4 (April 1940): 52–53.

In an article about milk, writer Elizabeth Frazer detailed the science of milk production from the consumer's point of view. She reported on an industrialist interested in producing condensed milk who decided he must have only healthy cows and clean methods of milking: "and because he made it profitable to the farmers, he could impose sanitary standards which were unheard of in his day." Frazer questioned a different industrialist about how he was able to get farmers to adhere to sanitary standards. The answer was that the farmers adhered to standards because it was profitable to do so. Here is a clue about the role of farming for the *Good Housekeeping* audience: farmers are producers and businessmen who must be educated to see profit in applying the best health standards before they would implement such standards voluntarily. Farm women are not visible to the consumer as participants in this process, however. When Frazer mentions women, late in the article, it is in the context of wishing that women all over the country could see the immaculate room in which cows were milked at one of the farms on her tour. Milk produced in such clean conditions and under such scientific standards, she wrote, was more expensive, but "the housewife who buys these quality products gets full value for her money."[26]

Two articles in the "How America Lives" feature in *Ladies' Home Journal* in 1955 and in 1960 focused on farm families.[27] One profiled a Washington State apple farm and its mistress, a city girl who had moved to the country. The other, in 1960, told of a migrant family that followed crops. Both stressed the hard work involved in farming life, even as they idealized the plain living and peacefulness of farming.[28] Gladys Taber's "Diary of Domesticity" continued to offer a rosy view of rural living. But the caveat that farm life is hard work also was emphasized through

26. Frazer, "Drink It Down or Eat It Up," *Good Housekeeping* 100:6 (June 1935): 92–93, 192ff.

27. Scholar Nancy A. Walker noted that despite the avowed purpose of the series to explore the economic and geographic diversity of the country as a whole, the articles tended to espouse a collection of values. "Rich or poor, urban or rural, of French or Dutch or Italian ancestry, all of the families profiled espoused a belief in hard work, honesty, frugality, humility, and the rewards that American society promised those who practiced such values" ("The *Ladies' Home Journal,* 'How America Lives,' and the Limits of Cultural Diversity," *Media History* 6:2 [February 2000]: 129).

28. Jan Weyl, "More Time for Living," *Ladies' Home Journal,* April 1955, 169ff.; Nelle Keys Bell, "Rich in Living Is Their Harvest," *Ladies' Home Journal,* August 1960, 121ff.

articles on migrant workers and crop pickers that portrayed their lives as part of an unceasing cycle of hard labor.[29]

The opposition of farm life to city life, of farmer to consumer, of farm woman to city woman, evident particularly in *Ladies' Home Journal* and *Good Housekeeping,* was manifested through content that characterized farm, rural, and country women as unfashionable and undesirable, even as it constructed farm women as wise and rich in common sense. The competing perspectives of farm life, along with a direct characterization of farmers as enemies of the consumer, underscored a division between two distinct cultures with borders that sharpened during the fifty years from 1910 to 1960.

Women as Citizens

Despite the contrast between city and farm women, a contrast that strengthened over the period studied, women as a group were treated in substantially the same ways even when citizenship, engagement with civic affairs and politics, became a national women's issue. When discussing women's citizenship, voting rights, and politics, the editors of all three mainstream magazines studied appeared to treat women as a monolithic group with similar interests. Editors of all three publications also treated woman suffrage and women's politics in similar ways; women's political issues were constructed as those surrounding their particular domain of domesticity and child, maternal, and public health.

In the months before the Nineteenth Amendment was ratified in August 1920, a construction of women as social citizens—that is, as members of communities who exercised power through social interactions, using social mores as weapons—was evident in the pages of *Ladies' Home Journal* studied. Here, women were constructed as ready to take on the world of politics and clean house—metaphorically and, perhaps, literally. These words from the editor in March 1920 illustrate: "Women specialize in keeping the house neat and ought to prove adept at cleaning our political house. More power to their brooms! On with the ceremony! Let them shake the dust off from a few of our political fixtures and see what is underneath. Let them drive the rats out of the public pantry."[30] Yet there

29. Margaret Hickey, "Crop Pickers Dilemma" and "When Migrant Children Arrive . . . ," *Ladies' Home Journal,* January 1955, 21, 137.

30. "The Editor's Page," *Ladies' Home Journal,* March 1920, 1.

were still questions about what women planned to do with suffrage. The title of an article in the same issue asked, "What Do Women Want with the Vote?" The final answer was simple: "To make American citizens, men and women, care more how they are governed. To redeem the vote from the effects of the long indifference of voters, and restore it to every man and woman in its full value as the sign and seal of democracy."[31]

Citizenship, apart from its meaning as participation in civic affairs and voting, also appeared to mean, for women, activism on behalf of women's issues. Farm women were included in these discussions, as producers of food for public consumption. In a September 1920 article, a "Farmer's Wife" wrote about making a home on the farm. A key part of the article is a demonstration of the standards of cleanliness required for scalding milking equipment. "You have to scald with water that is galloping if you want a reputation for milk that will keep," she noted.[32] *Reputation,* a key word here, refers to the farm woman's impression upon the world and the people around her, the informal yet enforced value of her work and life, which could then be translated into influence on others. In short, reputation meant a kind of social capital that, for farm women, also could be enacted as business capital.

The editor of *Good Housekeeping,* William Frederick Bigelow, seemed only to wait for the vote to be a near-reality before actively seeking the support of his readers for voter initiatives in 1920. In particular, Bigelow sought reader support for a bill he was advocating to Congress: the Sheppard-Towner Bill "for the public protection of maternity and infancy." An article by Rose Wilder Lane in the same issue explained some of the harsh statistics that revealed conditions under which women and infants died in childbirth across the United States. One of the most startling facts reported was that more than 125,000 babies each year died before they were six weeks old. Bigelow told readers, "The mothers of this country would pay two million dollars just to keep one grave from being dug—and in the hands of mothers is the power to make this bill a law." He added, "We all know that deficits can be made up, but none knows so well as mothers that arms, once emptied, can not be filled again."[33]

31. Esther Everette Lape, "What Do Women Want with the Vote?" *Ladies' Home Journal,* March 1920, 3, 91ff., 94.

32. A Farmer's Wife, "Making a Home on a Farm," *Ladies' Home Journal,* September 1920, 21, 131ff., 21.

33. Bigelow, "What the Editor Has to Say: *If You Want This Bill, Say So,*" *Good Housekeeping* 70:3 (March 1920): 4.

Advocacy for women's issues was at the center of the coverage in the 1925 issues of *Good Housekeeping* read as well. In the January issue, writing a feature in the form of an open letter to women, Frances Parkinson Keyes asserted that citizenship means, first of all, voting; but it also means participating in politics, engaging in "civic housekeeping" by helping to oust political leaders as necessary, and engaging with local community affairs and organizations.[34] In another item in the same issue, Bigelow advocated a child labor amendment. A woman judge, Florence E. Allen, stressed the importance of couples "making over" marriage rather than receiving quick divorces and urged women to learn something about civics and politics. This suggests a view that women still required education to understand their roles as citizens.[35]

Articles read in *Good Housekeeping* in 1930 stressed the need for improving social conditions, apparently as a method of inspiring readers to go about changing them. For example, Helen Buckler wrote about the physical conditions of county jails, in which men, women, and children all were held. Her article detailed the horrendous problems of physical and moral filth and decay.[36]

Articles read in 1935 issues of *Good Housekeeping* reveal a possible divergence from civic concerns on the part of the editors. The magazine's writers urged action on maternal health and child welfare bills before Congress, but nonfiction articles stressed homemaking and child rearing. No letters from readers, a dominant feature in the issues read from 1910 to 1930, were seen in 1935 issues read. In his editorial in June 1935, Bigelow discussed the challenge facing college students in what he called the "lost generation" in an America that seemed defeated and lost

34. Keyes, "Now that the Election Is Over—", *Good Housekeeping* 80:1 (January 1925): 35, 116ff. In an autobiographical sketch she wrote for a Catholic publication, Keyes credited her long period as mistress of a farm in New Hampshire for her success as a writer. "However, it is my firm belief that there can be no true vocation without a long novitiate and those unbroken years at the Farm formed a valuable period of apprenticeship for me. Despite the fact that I was the companion, as well as a nurse and teacher to my children, there were very few days when I did not manage to write a little" ("Frances Parkinson Keyes," http://www.catholicauthors.com/keyes.html, accessed 2008).

35. Bigelow, "Signboards and Guideposts," *Good Housekeeping* 81:4 (October 1925): 4; "What the Judges Told Us About Divorce," *Good Housekeeping* 80:4 (April 1925): 28–29; 156ff.; Judge Florence E. Allen, "A Charge to Woman Voters," *Good Housekeeping* 81:4 (October 1925): 19, 186ff.

36. Buckler, "Attack the County Jail," *Good Housekeeping* 91:2 (August 1930): 48–49, 144ff.

after the devastating Great Depression. "The point of it all," he wrote, "is that there is a new America in the making, and that it desperately needs to be made right this time in order that the suffering of the last few years may never have to be endured again."[37]

The September 1940 installment of Eleanor Roosevelt's three-part series on women in politics was printed near a guest editorial by Margaret Culkin Banning. Banning was indignant that seven states had already restricted, via legislation, the right of married women to work. "To make new laws or to uphold unwritten ones that do not allow married women to work is cutting at the roots of our civilization," she wrote. She continued:

> We want and need people in their jobs who are good at them. It is utterly wrong and unfair to turn out a married woman, who possibly supports her husband and several relatives, and to put in her job some girl who might do the work only half as well and who no doubt will get married as soon as she can. Unless, warned by the experience of the other woman, the girl thinks it is a better bet not to get married, but to keep her emotional and sexual life off the record. That is what is indirectly encouraged by many of these proposed laws. And what will that do to the birth rate among the competent?[38]

Women's citizenship—again treated as a characteristic of women as a monolithic group—also dominated the 1940 and 1945 issues of *Ladies' Home Journal* studied. Major articles were filled with war news. The overall impression today's reader gets from the stories and letters is of crisis, one in which women were uncertain about their traditional roles of home and child care. Dorothy Thompson, for example, wrote in February 1945 about the problems of marital infidelity when spouses are separated by war: "In fact, the gamut of questions [submitted to a radio show she hosted] reveals a sense of family insecurity arising out of the war, and an apprehension that it will be difficult, if not impossible, to stabilize it again."[39]

Moreover, the kinds of civic engagement women were encouraged to take part in were limited. Thompson wrote in July 1940 that attention to world affairs could go only so far; attention to everyday life was needed:

37. Bigelow, "Challenge," *Good Housekeeping* 100:6 (June 1935): 4.
38. Banning, "Wanted . . . All Women," *Good Housekeeping* 111:3 (September 1940): 21.
39. Thompson, "The Soldier's Wife," *Ladies' Home Journal*, February 1945, 6.

"I am afraid that I think that there is too much superficial discussion of vast world problems, and not enough attention paid to the matter of making everyday life more attractive." In separate paragraphs, Thompson wrote that public civilizations would rise and fall, and that wars would come and go, but the work women could do to create a nice garden and a beautiful home would be valued forever. She continued:

> It is a noble thing to save mankind, but it is also a contribution to humanity to be able to bake a good coconut cake or a first-rate apple pie. No civilization can stand more than one Joan of Arc at a time, but it can do with an almost unlimited number of good cooks. I doubt whether all the papers read in all the women's clubs on world organization for peace will stop men from killing one another in war, but women's clubs could help stop themselves, their husbands and their children from killing themselves and one another by reckless driving on the highroads. Anything that increases consideration for human life helps toward the eventual abolishing of war; anything that makes life more beautiful makes it more tolerable; and whatever develops resources inside ourselves—whether from eighteenth-century poetry or twentieth-century cookery—adds to human courage.[40]

In other words, Thompson wanted women to value their own possible contributions to global affairs by paying attention to their domestic pursuits and acting locally for the good of their communities. At the same time, reports by Ruth Drummond humanized the war in Europe, especially one in which she detailed her children's flight from wartorn England. Her personal letters appeared on the editor's page and elsewhere in the *Ladies' Home Journal.*

For both *Good Housekeeping* and *Ladies' Home Journal,* the issues read for 1945 focused on men returning from the war and what women could do to help them. In *Ladies' Home Journal,* editorials and letters from readers—which now seemed to be a mainstay of the publication, judging from the issues read—discussed women's roles in this new, postwar era. A series called "If I were a woman . . . If I were a man," featuring debates between notable men and women, was similar in format to the debates between "The Country Contributor" and "A Daughter of the City" in 1915. Gladys Taber's "Diary of Domesticity" was the only content for the rural woman. It is probable that the most prevalent issues treated

40. Thompson, "It's a Woman's World," *Ladies' Home Journal,* July 1940, 25.

for women—helping husbands readjust to civilian life, learning to live with a man who had been changed by his experiences in war—were universal for American women in this immediate postwar period.

In the 1945 issues of *Good Housekeeping* read, no discussion was found about women's citizenship, working women, or even food safety. Instead, fashions, homemaking, child rearing, and romantic fiction dominated editorial content. No letters from readers were found, and a new editor, Herbert R. Mayes, had control of content that pointedly directed women toward home concerns. No discussion of politics was found at all. This contrasts starkly with the dynamic civic debate and calls to public action seen in issues from previous years.

The issues of *Ladies' Home Journal* and *Good Housekeeping* read from 1950 stressed beauty, fashions, needlework, homemaking, and women's health. Baby departments focused on questions about child development; articles also discussed fertility. Since 1950 was the height of the postwar period known as the Baby Boom, this content, aimed at helping women cope with their growing families, is not surprising. But, again, civic discourse is absent. Today's reader might assume that women of that era were concerned only with life in the home. In *Good Housekeeping,* no readers' letters were found. In the same year, the issues of *Ladies' Home Journal* read focused particularly on babies—how to conceive them, how to take care of them, how to raise them "correctly" with advice from experts, even how to give birth properly. Frank discussions about women's bodies and sex, women's health and anxieties, and an emphasis on homemaking seem to depict women taking a step backward from civic engagement and public service. Where civic responsibility was touted, it was in editorials by Dorothy Thompson, such as "Community Begins at Home." This editorial counseled young families to involve their children in family decisions and crises rather than protecting children from them.[41] Although women were encouraged to think civically through columns by Dorothy Thompson and through timely articles by Margaret Hickey, what was printed in the magazine during this year focused more exclusively on homemaking and child rearing than had the content studied in previous years.

In 1960 issues examined from *Ladies' Home Journal,* articles were more conspicuously directed toward women's roles in civic affairs than in pre-

41. Thompson, "Community Begins at Home," *Ladies' Home Journal,* December 1950, 11–12, 168.

vious years. The matters with which women were expected to engage fell into the traditionally female arena—homemaking, child education, women's health—but readers' efforts to inform and be informed about such public issues were clear in each magazine studied. In 1960, attention was paid as well to urban and rural life throughout the magazines, and farm life was portrayed more positively, even in an article regarding migrant farmers for "How America Lives."[42]

In issues of *Good Housekeeping* read for 1955 and 1960, in contrast, it appeared that the editors assumed that readers did not care for discussion of civic matters. An April 1955 article featured the life of a senator's wife, and readers were assured in the table of contents: "No politics involved in this—just human interest." The article, which described the varied harried moments of public life and preparation for them, concluded with Nancy Kefauver describing a moment in which she was holding a hat on her head with one hand and her skirt down with the other, while people thrust bouquets of flowers in her face and her husband shouted for her to shake hands with the constituents. "That was the only time I completely forgot my Scottish background and wished that it was the wife who wore the pants in the family!" Kefauver wrote.[43] Thus, today's reader perceives that even a woman who spent her life in the political arena was compelled to reinforce her husband's dominance.

In 1960, letters from readers were found in the issues of *Good Housekeeping* studied. But discussion of civic matters and of women working outside the home was not seen.

As a whole, the content of these three mainstream magazines suggests that women in general were constructed as citizens who might best put their skills to work in advocating for issues traditionally seen as domestic, such as child education, public health, and women's health.

Farm Women and the Business of Farming

While *Good Housekeeping* did not address farm women per se, content in *Ladies' Home Journal* and *Saturday Evening Post* treated farm women in ways that addressed their business acumen as well as their centrality to the farm business. Farm women were often constructed as entrepreneurs, many

42. Nelle Keys Bell, "Rich in Living Is Their Harvest," *Ladies' Home Journal*, August 1960, 121ff.

43. "Mrs. Senator," *Good Housekeeping* 140:4 (April 1955): 58–61, 164ff. (168).

of whom worked in tandem with their husbands in the running of the farm business. The centrality of women to the success of farm businesses also was emphasized, predominantly in *Post* articles and editorials.

As farmers, women were discussed as vital, particularly in a series of articles directed toward farm women written by Annie E. P. Searing for *Ladies' Home Journal.* While the theme of farm women moving to cities is well expressed in the series, Searing wrote that women were more than capable farmers whose work was intrinsically valuable to the farm business: "The farm is the place of all the world of activity where feminine and masculine qualities can most beneficially intermingle, and the result be a good business investment."[44]

The entrepreneurial spirit of women in general was celebrated in the February 1915 issue of *Ladies' Home Journal* in women's letters addressing the subject of "how I helped my husband to make more money."[45] The letters, written in response to a query by the editors, were judged competitively. A Minnesota doctor's wife won top honors for her story about creating a rest home for farm women, a place where they could stay and be cared for by her husband and local nursing staff. The service, she explained, was used particularly when farm women were ill and their husbands brought them to the home in town for room, board, and care. A social room in the home was used regularly by visitors, family, and friends and by farm women who accompanied their husbands into town and did not want to wait for them in their wagons. "I have many cherished memories of friendships formed with these intelligent, wholesome women from the farms," she wrote.[46]

The word *wholesome* was used by an entrepreneurial Massachusetts farm woman to describe her produce in a letter about her business. She had learned of a process in England for drying and repackaging produce for sale as stew or soup mixes. She gathered several of her neighbors together and launched a company to process their own farm garden produce in this way and sell it. She reported that the products "sell well, even in the summertime, as they mean a distinct saving for the

44. Searing, "What Can I Do on the Farm?" *Ladies' Home Journal,* May 1915, 48.

45. "How I Helped My Husband to Make More Money," *Ladies' Home Journal,* February 1915, 33.

46. "$5000 the First Year for My Doctor-Husband," *Ladies' Home Journal,* February 1915, 33.

housewife and are quite as wholesome and nutritious as vegetables fresh from the farm in their natural state."[47]

Farming methods, financing, and progress were subjects of articles in the *Saturday Evening Post,* and each in some way mentioned the farmer's wife as pivotal to the success of the farming business. Her trustworthiness in business was noted and admired. For example, one article discussed loaning money to farmers. "The safest loan is that made to the homemaker," said the author, a banker. "If the wife signs the note I feel sure it will be paid. She will find some way to meet the obligation."[48]

Another point clearly made in a 1920 *Ladies' Home Journal* article by a "A Farmer's Wife" is that the farm business was a joint adventure of a man and a woman.

> Farmer and wife are partners literally from the ground up if they are the right sort of people, intimately associated in all their work both inside and outside the house in a way that few other husbands and wives have to be. Some women say they don't care to know anything about their husband's business so long as the money comes in. I have even heard that some boast they do not know what their husbands' business is! No doubt it proves a satisfactory arrangement to both parties in their line of work.
>
> But that attitude in a farmer's wife would be ruinous. To be a success, their work must go hand in hand. There can be no operations, business secrets or dealings with somebody outside that one of the partners does not understand and knows nothing about. Everything in their daily lives is an open book between them.[49]

The statement that farm women can and must act as equal partners with their spouses in the running of the farm business contrasts with the domestic roles described for city women, who are characterized as uninterested in their husbands' businesses. The sphere of the farm woman included a variety of tasks and interactions that moved beyond the home.

The importance of women to business and to civics also was a significant topic of discussion, particularly on the *Post*'s editorial pages. Editor

47. "This Wife Opened Up a New Way to Make Money," *Ladies' Home Journal,* February 1915, 33.

48. Charles Moreau Harger, "The Farmer and His Bank," *Saturday Evening Post* 182:42 (April 16, 1910): 25.

49. A Farmer's Wife, "Making a Home on a Farm," *Ladies' Home Journal,* September 1920, 21, 131ff.

George Horace Lorimer suggested in 1915 that women in general were being educated to be social ornaments rather than useful contributors to society. "Practically," Lorimer wrote, "she meets more incentives to do her hair prettily than to develop her mind." Her mind, he said, could be developed to be useful to society through education. He concluded: "We do not think any fair-minded person who takes stock of the charming women of his acquaintance will deny that a considerable portion of the world's brain power is practically unused. In view of the muddle the world gets into with what brain power it does practically use, this seems a large preventable loss."[50]

Elizabeth Frazer, whose byline also appeared in *Good Housekeeping*, reported about women's political issues and wrote guest editorials from the women's perspective for *Saturday Evening Post* in 1920. Her reporting continued in 1925 issues read for this research. Frazer addressed such issues as child labor and education. Her presence suggests that business leaders were receptive to women authors. Other articles read from 1925 exalted women's accomplishments in the United States, and still others addressed farm businesses and conditions in a way that placed the farm woman as central to the success of a farm. Unease over farm financing began to be apparent from issue to issue, as editorials and articles discussed varied methods of helping the farmer stay in business.

In 1930, as the Great Depression began, less big-business boosterism was seen in issues read. The *Saturday Evening Post* was fewer pages. Although it had fewer pages, it had better quality illustrations, some photos, and a good use of color on some pages. Farming was not exactly in the background as articles addressed the foreclosures of family farms, but the *Saturday Evening Post*'s editors may have found it hard to be positive about a business that seemed to be going "bust." Articles addressed the growing problem of unemployment, and some provided advice about weathering poor business conditions. An antilabor ideology became more pronounced in 1930 issues read. Editor Lorimer cautioned readers to gain all the facts about unemployment before taking action to support government interference in business practices:

> No subject so lends itself to oratorical discussion and display as unemployment. It is something which we all deplore and admit to be a blot upon civilization. Obviously, if the affairs of mankind were managed perfectly no one would be out of work except those who could not work.

50. Lorimer, "Using Women's Brains," *Saturday Evening Post* 187:45 (May 8, 1915): 26.

> Whenever there is an increase in the number of those without jobs, this hoary fact is dressed up anew and made much of. Unemployment has mounted since last summer; there can be no shadow of doubt about that. The slump in stocks had at least a temporarily chilling effect upon certain lines of business, and employment figures dropped off. Upon these facts all are agreed. But how much has unemployment declined? Was it serious in December and January? Has it become better or worse since then? . . . Unemployment can be banished from the country not by hysterical denunciations of it but by getting at the facts and acting upon them.[51]

The unemployment theme became more prevalent in issues read, as did a theme of immigrants taking jobs from Americans.

In the 1935 issues of the *Saturday Evening Post* read, many bylines for women writers were seen more often. Some articles addressed farming conditions and problems that may not have been as evident to Americans in 1930. Victoria Hazelton wrote about work relief programs and the tangible results that she saw. Others related the classic rags-to-riches story of capitalism. "From Farm Boy to Financier," for example, told of a young man who worked himself into wealth.[52] Other articles addressed what farmers could do to keep their farms during the economic crisis, and others appear to have been intended to explain away the horrible economic conditions by calling those who were unemployed victims of a "pink slip strike" or of excessive taxation of the wealthy, who clearly opposed New Deal politics. On the editorial page, Lorimer, in a tone that could be considered antilabor, argued that capital in the hands of big business could create more jobs and opportunities. He wrote about readers' letters asserting that profits from stock dividends earned by corporations should be given back to workers. Lorimer opposed that view. He used one letter, which suggested that a fourth of all such profit should be directly distributed to labor, to refute such arguments:

> This is too moderate a letter to be representative of one large section of any editor's mail since 1929; a correspondence angry in the belief that, as we were rich then and are poor now, someone must have the missing wealth; that as labor certainly hasn't it, capital must. But its very moderation makes it that much more striking. For, reasonable as it may sound, it starts with an error of 100 per cent and compounds it.[53]

51. Lorimer, "Unemployment," *Saturday Evening Post* 202:44 (May 3, 1930): 32.
52. Frank A. Vanderlip and Boyden S. Parkes, "From Farm Boy to Financier," *Saturday Evening Post* 207:36 (March 9, 1935): 29.
53. Lorimer, "We Do Deny," *Saturday Evening Post* 207:36 (March 9, 1935): 22.

Regarding farm life, some editorials acknowledged the drought that had led to many farm foreclosures but noted that drought is a condition of life that could not have been anticipated. "If good rains come every third or fourth year, the farmer has made enough to carry him over the dry spells. He has gambled with his eyes open," Lorimer wrote in the June 1, 1935, issue.[54] In the same issue, an article about the negative effect of government interference in charging more for wheat going overseas explained the resulting oversupply in Europe from 1929 to 1933. "In attempting to make the marginal farmer prosperous, the prosperity of the rest of the farmers was seriously impaired," wrote Putnam Dana McMillan. He added that such farmers had gone into debt to mechanize their farms in search of higher profits but ultimately had lost everything.[55]

Much content seen in 1935 issues justified and explained business conditions under which millions within the United States were suffering, and the farming business was part of that discussion. The solution to the economic depression, according to *Saturday Evening Post* editorials, was not the New Deal; the solution was freeing capital for investments in big business to create more jobs and lowering farm production and pricing to cut down on supply.

The *Saturday Evening Post* issues studied in 1940 discussed the war in Europe and speculated about whether the United States would join the war. The importance of outdoor sports to the American people was also discussed, and articles about sporting events were seen for the first time. Discussion in the 1940 and 1945 issues portrayed big business positively and offered strategies for succeeding in such businesses as farming. Capitalism was treated as the best and only way to succeed in life. It is telling that during this period, in 1936, Rose Wilder Lane published "Credo," a treatise boosting capitalism and Americanism, in the *Saturday Evening Post.*

In the issues studied from 1945, articles discussed what soldiers would do once they came home as well as the rebuilding of Europe—and the economics of doing so. Profiles of industrialists were also seen, and farming businesses, called "ranches," were discussed. In articles about the latter, farm women were mentioned briefly, in the context of their roles in building successful businesses.

54. Lorimer, "'It Always Has Rained,'" *Saturday Evening Post* 207:48 (June 1, 1935): 26.

55. McMillan, "Marginal Land and Marginal Thinking," *Saturday Evening Post* 207:48 (June 1, 1935): 27, 88ff.

In 1950, content in the magazine issues read centered on urban culture and the cold war anticommunist ideology. Strategies to succeed in business were not found. The rhetoric reflected increasing hostility toward anything seen as socialist or communist—including organized labor—and the view that the ideals of a capitalist society were the only "real" ideals. The *Saturday Evening Post,* of course, had history as a booster of big business. Farming was not mentioned as often as in issues studied from earlier years, but the illustrations on the magazine's front cover and in some advertising continued to show pastoral scenes of rolling hills and pink-cheeked children. More articles within the magazine also addressed how people moving to the cities from farming areas could adjust to city life. This suggests that the editors assumed that those raised on farms needed such instruction, and that American city life was as foreign to them as was any other country.

In 1955 issues studied, less discussion was found of farming as a business, but a recurring theme in features about industrialists and business leaders was their early lives as farm youth. Such references to a farm upbringing suggest that those who now lived in the cities—primarily entrepreneurs—looked back on that upbringing with the rosy tint of nostalgia. One might also read into such references the idea that farm life is good training for those who would succeed in business.

In the 1960 issues of the *Saturday Evening Post* read, urban society was the focus of a series of articles, "Our Urban Evolution," which highlighted a rural-to-urban movement that had been documented in the magazine over the previous fifty years. Farming had been a serious, significant business in 1910, but as the years passed, with war, depression, drought, and the mechanization of the farm businesses, more people who had been farmers lived in the city than on farms. More urbanites were moving into the suburbs for a life they hoped would balance a need for country spaces against the need for city employment.

The *Saturday Evening Post* issues read showed the magazine to have been a booster of big business from the beginning to the end of the period under study, and the farming business was a significant subject in its content. Farm women were discussed as capable businesswomen who were significant to the success of farm businesses. Women in general were discussed as capable and competent within their own domestic domains. As time wore on, magazine content continued to be ideologically conservative, against government interference, and pro-capitalist. These stances may have been emphasized more during the cold war of the 1950s than at other times, but they were an inherent part of all the issues of the magazine that were studied for this book.

Study of selected issues from selected years of *Ladies' Home Journal*, *Good Housekeeping*, and *Saturday Evening Post* showed that, while women in general were treated differently among the magazines, farm women were treated remarkably similarly. Farm women were discussed as businesswomen, and their presence on farms was treated as directly relevant to farming success. Farm women were written about as primary producers of food for consumers, and they were discussed as women who could and did make solid contributions to civic life.

But how did these themes play out in farming magazines? Given the apparent divide between rural and urban women, how were farm women constructed in media aimed directly at their households? The mainstream magazines provided a solid introduction to national society and constructions of women, of whom farm women were a part, and help ground us in that history. But finding the culture of farm women requires a longer look at the farming magazines that addressed their particular worlds.

4

A Message to Farm Women
Consider "How Unique You Are"

"First of all, we raised everything we ate," Dorothy Fehrenbach, of Cincinnati, Ohio, wrote.

> We raised all our vegetables and all the excess was canned and put in the cellar, so we had vegetables all winter. You see the cellar had no heat because we didn't have a furnace, we heated with wood burning stoves in the living room and a cook stove in the kitchen. The cellar was underground so it was always cool in the summer and warm in the winter.
>
> We raised pigs, so in the winter time we butchered our hogs and made all kinds of sausage, pork chops, ham, lard, bacon. We had cows, so we always had fresh milk everyday. We had a separator so we could separate the cream from the milk. Cream was made into butter and the milk was made into cottage cheese.
>
> We had some fruit trees, apple, cherry and peach and a lot of blackberries. We canned the fruit also in the summer just like we did the vegetables. We had a lot of woods on the farm, so in the winter when the weather was fair the men cut down trees and sawed up the limbs for firewood.
>
> We made all our bread and coffee cake. So you see that was a great advantage living on a farm. You had all the food you wanted and you didn't have to buy it. We only went to town when we needed shoes and needed a dress for a special occasion. Most of our everyday dresses were homemade, and we bought the material in town.[1]

Fehrenbach's story illustrates the bedrock notions of a successful farm: one that sustains itself and provides all the family needs to live well. Farm publications from 1910 to 1960 demonstrated the value of this kind of farming, even as the magazines underwent significant changes due to many national trends affecting farm life, including a growing exodus of rural readers to urban areas. These magazines were forced to cut subscription costs, to merge, and to shift content in efforts to stay in business. *Farm Journal*, a monthly, remains the only significant

1. Dorothy Fehrenbach, Cincinnati, Ohio, letter to author, February 7, 2007.

national magazine directed to a farming audience. *The Farmer's Wife,* first published in 1897 by Webb Publishing Company in St. Paul, Minnesota, was sold to *Farm Journal* in 1939, and it was then bound into the back of the magazine under its own cover until 1970. *Country Gentleman,* renamed *Better Living* in 1955, ended in August 1955, when it also was sold to *Farm Journal.* All three publications remained more or less intact through the years encompassed by this research. Each was studied to determine how it presented farm women as women, as citizens, and as farmers.

While differences in editorial philosophy among the magazines could be seen, farm women were constructed in substantially similar ways: as the architects of farm life and keepers of the farm home and as important and central to the business of farming. These two constructions did not change substantially over the fifty-year period encompassed here. Farm women's citizenship—as participation in politics and voting—was seen as an accepted right. This was likely due to women's centrality to the farm home and farm business, and to the respect that the farm community, as represented through these magazines, had for these women.

Some Notes about the Farm Magazines

As the only national magazine that directly addressed farm women as a group, *The Farmer's Wife* is a rich source of information about farm women in the United States, particularly until its merger with *Farm Journal* in 1939. This magazine differs from both the traditional woman's magazine and the farmer's magazine in that it served both as a resource for farm women and as a medium through which they could communicate with each other. *The Farmer's Wife* featured women's news and three separate columns of readers' letters, each of which generated lively discussion on a variety of topics. These letters, a remarkable source for those seeking out farm women's thoughts, are discussed in greater detail in the next chapter.

Practical domestic content appears in the front of each issue of *The Farmer's Wife;* departments—including sections on poultry, dairy, garden produce, clothing, and cooking—are in the back. Editorials, which are in prominent positions, feature news and opinions on politics, business, and national issues of interest to farm women. Editors offered information and advice they apparently believed farm women could use, and the topics were not only for homemakers and child rearers but also for businesswomen and citizens. The greatest emphases were on farm women as important to the family farm business and home and as capable and competent people. That their capabilities were seen as extending to substantial skill in financial management and entrepreneurship was evident throughout the entire period encompassed by this research.

Previous research, discussed here in tandem with *The Farmer's Wife* material, focused on the period between 1910 and 1926 by individual year. Examples from that research thus reflect all those years and not just the five-year intervals from 1910 to 1926.[2]

Content in the *Country Gentleman* was directed at the whole farm family. The issues studied across the entire 1910–1955 period provide information about farming conditions and pricing, farming methods and progress, state and federal politics as applied to farming, and farm family life. Content more explicitly related to farm businesses was found in the first pages of the issues studied, but prominent sections on domestic economy and science, along with the numerous women contributors to the business content, suggest that the farm woman was central to the audience that *Country Gentleman*'s editors sought to reach. By 1955, most of the demonstrably "feminine" content was found in *Country Gentlewoman,* bound into the back of *Country Gentleman.* However, from issue to issue in those studied from 1910 to 1955, women writers contributed bylined stories to the magazine's regular content.

Farm Journal also stressed women's contributions to the farm business, and in all the issues studied the farm home was treated as central to the success of the farm business. In all of those issues, *Farm Journal* also featured women writers and women's advice on varying aspects of the farming business. Farm families were also central, even after the mergers of *Farm Journal* with *The Farmer's Wife* in 1939 and with *Country Gentleman* in 1955. On the whole, one perceives in the magazine's content a farm culture of life and business as intertwined, with women at the heart of that relationship.

"How Unique You Are"

Respect for girls and women was seen in 1910 *Farm Journal* articles that directly addressed farm men about how they treated the women who worked alongside them. "Have you told her what a blessing she is

2. This research was presented at the American Journalism Historians Association annual conference in 2003 as "The Voice of *The Farmer's Wife:* Wife, Mother, Citizen, Businesswoman, 1911–1926."

to you?" Farmer Vincent asked, pointing to the pride of farm men in the goods produced by farm women for sale.[3] It appears that the editors of *Farm Journal* may have thought change was necessary to keep women on the farms.

That respect, also seen in subsequent issues of all three farm magazines studied, is highlighted in times of farming crises. The preoccupation with the politics of the New Deal and the economic crises that had swept the country likely helped limit discussion of farm women's concerns in *Farm Journal* issues studied from 1935. However, an emphasis on the farm home as the site for decision making and political discussion suggests that the business strands still converged there. A section titled "Home Department," introduced in 1935 by Mary R. Reynolds, offered farm women the chance to participate in their own section within the *Farm Journal.* In her introduction, Reynolds explained what she thought the farm woman needed and wanted—while inviting readers to write and tell her where she was wrong.

> By the way, did you ever stop to think how unique you are—how you compose the one large group of women in this country that has an opportunity to keep in touch with the business of their men, to know enough about their work to be interested in it and to talk intelligently with them about it? The average city woman has little opportunity to learn about the work of her husband. A farmer's wife is truly his partner.

She noted that farm women needed better and bigger recipes, with more detailed instructions, than did city women, who could rely on area bakers and delicatessens to help them. Farm women needed better strategies for helping their children find playmates and activities than did city women, whose children had ready access to many other children. And farm women, Reynolds wrote, did not need formal style information as much as they needed to know what the well-dressed woman was wearing "at home and on the street."[4]

In the January 1935 issue of *The Farmer's Wife,* an editorial reminded farm women—and farm men—of women's importance to keeping the farming community together. In "A Testimony Meeting," editors discussed a gathering of farm men who talked about farm women:

3. Farmer Vincent, "Is She Your Wife?" *Farm Journal* 39:8 (August 1915): 431.
4. Reynolds, "The Home," *Farm Journal* 59:10 (October 1935): 27, 38.

> Their talk turned from one thing to another and finally to the subject of what farm women had been doing to keep up morale in difficult times.
>
> "It was my wife who kept up the spirit of our family," said one man. And then testimony followed testimony. Farm women managed skillfully with less than enough; they kept homes looking well and saw that life within was cheerful; they and their neighbors maintained community activities; they held their husbands to continued faith in agriculture; they encouraged them to give the government full cooperation; they fulfilled the definition of home as a place with a world of love shut in and a world of strife shut out.
>
> We pass this story on to our readers, because husbands often seem reluctant to give praise to their wives.[5]

In acknowledging the demanding times of what would be known as the Great Depression, a period when drought conditions made farming difficult and economic hardships were known across the United States, the editors wrote that it was farm women who were keeping families together and keeping the faith in the farming business. By 1940, *The Farmer's Wife* had merged with *Farm Journal* in response to economic conditions. But the construction of the farm woman as central to the farm home, an architect of its success, remained.

In 1950, a new subtitle on the *Country Gentleman* cover was "The magazine for better farming—better living." Content for and about women focused almost exclusively on fashion, family health, and homemaking. Nostalgia for the past, too, centering farm women at the heart of cherished family memories, was seen in 1950 as in 1945. Margaret Weymouth Jackson, writing a feature about a farm family at Christmas in December 1950, described Ina Mae Tolin, of Parke County, Indiana, as the ideal farm woman:

> Pretty, quiet, deeply sincere, she is a true farm woman, loves the land and the stock, the house and the children, the work and the worry. She has great courage, and for her children she wants good health and good characters, normal lives and usefulness. She is a woman who says "do" rather than "don't," who sometimes looks forward to the time when it will be just herself and Roy again, and who at other times tries to stay the hurrying years. Deeply maternal, she's a good mother in the best meaning of the word. She's a wonderful cook, a fair-to-middling housekeeper,

5. "A Testimony Meeting," *The Farmer's Wife,* January 1935, 3.

> and she has a knack for making everyone happy. She's just herself, and that has to be enough for friend or foe, if any, family and husband. And it is enough—pressed down and running over.[6]

She seems to see the true farm woman as embracing the land, the work, and the worry along with her house and her children; she can cook, but she may not be the best housekeeper. She also must be the cheerleader, seeing everyone else's needs, making them all happy, and, presumably, putting herself last. However, Jackson depicts her value to the farm home and business as being unparalleled—indeed, it is "pressed down and running over."

The Keepers of the Farm Home

The 1910 issues of *The Farmer's Wife* indicated that farm women were already strong voices for change in their communities. Two significant issues were education for rural youth and suffrage, both seen also in 1915 and in 1920. In January 1911, the editors told readers of a plan to feature successful farm women each month. This feature was seen in varied forms in issues read throughout the years under study. The articles focused on women who "have taken up claims in our great Western country, and have successfully met and conquered the discouragements and trials incident to such a life." The purpose of the regular features, according to the editors, was to deal "with some phase of work pertaining to women on a farm, all of which will be found of great interest. Stories, grave and gay, practical and deliciously full of love and fun, by well known authors, will appear each month to instruct and entertain."[7] Given the importance of women to the business of farming, the editors also expressed concern about reports of more women and girls leaving farms for lives in the city: "If your life has taught you anything, it is your business—note the word *business*—to use that knowledge for studying and planning better ways and means to help your daughter on in the duties you are turning over to her."[8]

It should be noted that daughters were expected to do mainly domestic work, including sewing, baking, and cleaning, but there was a discussion of the importance of education for farm women. "Parents

6. Jackson, "Farm Christmas," *Country Gentleman* 120:12 (December 1950): 28, 58ff.

7. "The Farmer's Wife for 1911," *The Farmer's Wife*, January 1911, 238.

8. "Girls and the Farm," *The Farmer's Wife*, January 1911, 238 (emphasis in original).

have no moral right to stand in the way of proper development and health of their children," Jessie Field, Page County, Iowa, superintendent of schools, wrote in January 1911. "When they do, to them, not the children, should be meted the punishment." Field described the kind of education country girls should have. Of the "three R's," she called arithmetic essential for girls who would be running farm accounts. In addition, Field wrote that country girls who would be managing farm households needed sewing and cooking classes. "The Mother's Club," a regular feature, also discussed farm girls' education. In one article, written in the form of a conversation among many women, Maude K. Goodwill listed several skills she thought should be taught to country girls and future farm women; these take into account the blurring through marriage of lines between rural and urban living. Girls, she wrote, should be taught how to make a home and care for it; how to choose a suitable mate; how to take care of their own health, because health was a farmwife's most useful asset; how to be brave in the face of difficulties; and how to maintain household accounts and understand finance. "The day is passing when a man can be a successful farm citizen without an intelligent woman as a partner," the editors noted in May 1912.[9]

Some items in *The Farmer's Wife* discussed men as blind to their wives' needs and needing reeducation to enable them to "see" their wives' value. Farm women were coached as to the best ways to enlighten their husbands about the value of a woman's work, health, and well-being. An example is an anecdote from October 1914:

> A man who had been obliged to do the housework during his wife's illness very much amused and surprised her by announcing that he was going to look into this "fireless cooker proposition." He said in a very bombastic manner, "This here puttering around and watching things cook is all nonsense. Start 'em cooking and put them in a box and when you want them they are ready." He had forgotten that after a third suggestion the previous summer in regard to this very subject he became sufficiently interested to remark, "Buying just such trash as that is the reason Bill Jones can't have an auto and I can." While there are many farmers in this class, it is, I believe, from a lack of interest and thought rather than from any other reasons.[10]

9. Field, "Educating Country Girls," *The Farmer's Wife*, January 1911, 244; Goodwill, "Our Girls: How to Train for Greatest Usefulness," *The Farmer's Wife*, April 1911, 324; "The Woman's Part," *The Farmer's Wife*, May 1912, 372.

10. Mildred M. Veitch, "North Dakota's Plan: Wiping Out Drudgery as an Answer to the Farm Woman's Problems," *The Farmer's Wife*, October 1914, 139.

Farm women were also discussed as capable of independent living, without men to help them out. Articles highlighted the successful farms of women without mates: "They Paid the Mortgage" and "We Three Women Kept the Farm: It Required Courage to Meet the Situation without Hired Help But We Have Won Out." Alice Wilson, one of the three women referred to in the second title, wrote in May 1921, "Ours is the satisfaction of having tackled a hard proposition and made good. There is always joy in that."[11]

The idea that women were central to the farm home and farm business was clear in 1915 issues of the *Country Gentleman* studied. A new feature, "Country Gentlewoman," was written entirely by women. Articles provided advice for preserving food, making clothing, and mending existing clothing so that it would last longer.[12] Articles discussed how Smith-Lever funds could directly benefit the farm woman. The Smith-Lever Act of 1914 had established cooperative extension agencies that, among other things, were to help provide education and training to farm women. One writer said such funds should be put to use in improving conditions in farm homes but added that such conditions would not improve without full support from the men of the household. "Say what you will, the question of how to assist the farm woman hangs largely for its solution upon the farmer who provides the living for that home," an unsigned writer explained. The same writer noted that Smith-Lever funds were to be used for education and other assistance that would help make "successes" of farm businesses.[13]

In the 1920 issues of *Country Gentleman* studied, the farm woman's centrality to the farm home and her importance to the farm business were highlighted even more with articles that advised farm women on running their businesses and features about specific farm homes. For example, a feature by Harry Snowden Stabler about the Ralston family of Rockingham County, Virginia, discussed the family's productivity and success at farming and paid special attention to Mrs. Ralston, whose work in the home and on the farm brought her joy as well as practical success. He wrote that her family seemed "to think her the biggest asset

11. Harry Botsford, "They Paid the Mortgage," *The Farmer's Wife,* July 1920, 56; Alice Wilson, "We Three Women Kept the Farm," *The Farmer's Wife,* May 1921, 444.

12. For one example, see Julia C. Gray, "Asparagus on a Town Lot," *Country Gentleman* 80:33 (August 14, 1915): 9.

13. "Progressive Agriculture: What the Government Is Doing for the Farmer's Business and Home," *Country Gentleman* 80:20 (May 15, 1915): 847.

they have."[14] A significant number of articles in 1920 were aimed at persuading farmers that labor-saving devices for the farm home were just as important to successful farming as any new farming machinery. This argument was obvious in articles, but it also was seen in advertising. One full-page advertisement for a Simplex ironing machine called it a means for "health, happiness and contentment for the farm woman." Two pictures at the top sell the machine; one features a clean, smiling woman using a Simplex ironing machine, and the other features a tired, worn-out woman ironing with old flatirons from the top of a cookstove. In the text, a "wise farmer" says that he intended to put some of his profits back into making life more pleasant for his wife and daughter. "The women on the farms have a hard time, and it's a good investment to keep them contented."[15]

The Business of Farm Women

The January 13, 1910, Fireside Department in *Country Gentleman* begins, "How One Woman Earned Money: Basket Willow on the Farm." The editor then introduces a lengthy letter from a farmer's daughter about her use of ten acres of poor land given to her when she decided to stay at home with her parents after college: "The question of earning money is one of the most practically important to the farmers' daughters. It may be said that there is quite enough for them to do in the farmhouse assisting their mother; but in nine cases out of ten they are dissatisfied unless they can make something of their own. If they can't do this on the farm, they are apt to leave it." The young woman's married older sisters had encouraged her to live on her own after college rather than stay on the farm with their parents. After thinking about the idea, the age of her parents, and the lack of other siblings on the farm, she decided to stay. Her father deeded to her ten acres of land, the poorest on the farm, which she turned into a basket willow grove from which she realized regular profit.[16]

This story suggests that *Country Gentleman* staff made efforts to show young farm women that they were valued and valuable to the farming community.

14. Stabler, "The Real Farm Home," *Country Gentleman* 85:11 (March 13, 1920): 52, 80–82.

15. Simplex Ironer ad, *Country Gentleman* 85:24 (June 12, 1920): 1.

16. "How One Woman Earned Money," *Country Gentleman* 75:2972 (January 13, 1910): 42.

The item also suggests respect for the success of one farm woman, and it shows that she could and did act as a successful entrepreneur.

In issue after issue, *Country Gentleman* included stories about women who succeeded in farm-related businesses, with special attention given to women who were running large farms on their own in innovative ways. For example, the success of Mary A. Brownell in doubling production at a dairy farm was explained in detail, with her innovations held up as examples for other farmers.[17] This and other articles demonstrated farm women's prowess in all aspects of the farming business. The use of the pronoun *we* by readers and writers in discussing farm methods and tips suggests that they did not consider the farming business to be the sole responsibility of the male farmer "in charge." For example, "We wish to get this field back into grass again, and the very best stand possible," wrote "Manager" in the April 7, 1910, issue. "We wanted to raise this water so as to submerge a Cooley can in it, and also to get it high enough to run into a trough," wrote D.B. in the same issue.[18] The consistent use of "we" in such letters calls to mind John Mack Farragher's assertion that the family was the unit of labor on the farm.[19]

Some feature articles in the 1915 issues of *Country Gentleman* studied detailed personal accounts of success in particular aspects of farm business; for example, "A Farmer's Wife" wrote about her success in raising turkeys. The instructional article details her procedures for helping young turkeys survive the first six weeks of their lives. "After that a minimum amount of work is required to look after the flock," she wrote. In the same issue, other women contributed items about dealing with crop pests and insects and the dangers and benefits of electricity and gas motors.[20] In a subsequent issue, women wrote about how to grow beans, install automatic henhouse doors, and plan meals when farms were miles from markets.[21]

17. "A Woman Who Succeeded," *Country Gentleman* 75:2984 (April 7, 1910): 353.

18. "For a Permanent Meadow" and "Casing for a Spring," *Country Gentleman* 75:2984 (April 7, 1910): 341.

19. Faragher, "History from the Inside-Out."

20. In *Country Gentleman* 80:6 (February 6, 1915): A Farmer's Wife, "How I Raised Turkeys: A Profitable Side Line for a Woman," 28; Ellen Robertson Miller, "Homes of Insects," 50; H. D. Jones, "The Silent Servant," 52.

21. In *Country Gentleman* 80:7 (February 13, 1915): Helen T. Woods, "The Automatic Hen House Door," 45; Harriette V. Davis, "Beans in Michigan," 46; Ida Bailey-Allen, "Ten Miles from a Market," 49.

It seems to have been understood at this time that many women were running the farm finances. Writer Ruth Dunbar, prominent in the 1920 issues of *Country Gentleman* studied, focused on particular business sidelines women could take up as well as on business courses women could take from home. Dunbar wrote about Cornell University courses sponsored by Martha Van Rensselaer, a pioneering home economist, whom Dunbar quoted as saying that farm women were the "biggest of big-business women," and that farm women were essential to the success of farming. Dunbar quoted Rensselaer further:

> More men all the time realize that they wouldn't have much of a farm without their heroic partners. So it's not only that women these days marry because they want to instead of because they have to; it's not only the shortage of farm wives; it's the whole industrial situation that's making the farmer look at his wife with new and keener and more considerate eyes. The national problem just now is agricultural. The agricultural problem is production. Here's where the big-business woman comes in. And here's where we come in with her—to try to help her meet her constantly changing needs.

In the same article, Dunbar discussed the importance of farm women making connections with each other. She wrote, for example, of gathering farm women together for discussions on how to improve their working conditions and understand their businesses better. In such gatherings, Dunbar noted, farm women could discuss politics: "For since the woman on the New York farm has the vote she intends to use it intelligently."[22]

In the 1925 issues of *Country Gentleman* studied, several women writers in addition to Dunbar were seen, including Emma Gertrude Roundy, Catherine Warren, Dorothy Canfield, Clara Ingram Judson, Amelia Leavitt Hill, Rose Wilder Lane, and Winnifred Kirkland. Each writer had a distinctive style and addressed unique topics, but a common theme was making money: how women could start their own businesses, keep their own accounts, and keep the money they made. A section about "Girls' Life" on farms provided advice to young women about how they, too, could make money to buy the things they wanted. The theme of

22. Ruth Dunbar, "The Biggest Big-Business Woman: College Courses at Home Help Her to Manage Better Her Department on the Farm," *Country Gentleman* 85:50 (December 11, 1920): 10–11.

farm women as central to the farm business remained dominant, and farm women also were written about as strong, independent businesswomen in their own right.

Discussions of farm women as successful entrepreneurs and businesswomen were seen throughout the issues of *The Farmer's Wife* studied. Each featured women had experienced remarkable success with some form of business, usually associated with farmwork. Poultry raising appeared to be the most prominent such business, but other ventures were beekeeping, fruit and vegetable gardening, cooking and canning, and boarding summer "guests" for income. Some articles concentrated on flower gardening and bulb raising, while others discussed livestock and dairying as good businesses for women.

Common to all these items was the idea that the primary ingredient for success was hard work. For example, a writer identified as Mrs. Brick attributed her successful poultry venture to hard work, not luck: "No, indeed, there is no luck about the successful chicken business; it is hard and some of it very disagreeable work. . . . To sum it all up, although the result of the first year's business does not show a large amount on the right side of the ledger, we feel satisfied with it, and are hopeful for the future." Another writer, who talked about lambing and gardening as ways to earn money, added: "Altogether, I believe the country girl has a much better chance than her city cousin to earn either pin-money or a competency, without special training or much capital. But she must not be afraid to work. She needs the same qualifications that any successful business person needs the world over."[23]

Farm women were discussed in many issues as the keepers of farm accounts and business. *The Farmer's Wife* editors conducted a contest for farm women to suggest the most practical plan of keeping farm home accounts. "We do not want theoretical or untried systems. We want something that someone has tried out and knows to be good," they wrote in the September 1913 issue.[24]

Women often wrote to editors and discussed their worth on the farm in terms of dollars and cents. "If we only study the question of supply and demand, we can turn many an honest penny without further trouble

23. Mrs. Brick, "A Successful Poultry Venture: Results from Hard, Persistent Work—Not Luck," *The Farmer's Wife,* October 1911, 134; Alice Margaret Ashton, "How the Farm Girl Can Earn Money," *The Farmer's Wife,* July 1914, 60.

24. "Household Accounts," *The Farmer's Wife,* September 1913, 118.

than the labor necessary to produce such things as the public desires and is willing to pay for," E. M. Ashley wrote in a July 1914 letter to the Home Club, a monthly column of readers' letters. A fiction story told of one farm woman tracking how much her hired man ate and putting monetary value on the farm produce and household goods used in preparing a meal as a means of placing a monetary value on herself and her work.[25]

When in 1930 the U.S. Census began to gather data for the profession of "homemaker," which included most farm women, the editors of *The Farmer's Wife* treated this action positively. In one editorial, they described the farm woman/homemaker:

> But it is worth while that the housewife be classed as a person of occupation, and it does make a difference. She makes a larger contribution to home building than the artisan who wields hammer and saw or trowel, and that is said without intending any disrespect to carpenter or brickmason. She builds with health, mind and soul values, and through them transforms a mere house into a home. There can not fail to be encouragement of self respect and satisfaction through recognition of the dignity of woman's work in the home.[26]

The magazine's emphasis on farm woman's importance to the farming business makes categorizing farm women as "homemakers" seem odd. Nevertheless, in 1930, the official acknowledgment of women whose primary work roles lay in the home was treated by the editors as a step toward publicly valuing women's work on farms.

By 1940, *Farm Journal* and *The Farmer's Wife* had merged and were bound together. Between 1940 and 1960, all the domestic content previously found in *Farm Journal* appeared in *The Farmer's Wife,* except for occasional articles highlighting farm families and farm family businesses. Mentions of farm women in *Farm Journal* stressed women as central to the running of the farm business and the farm home, the centrality of the farm family to the farm business, and women as capable, competent, and able "department heads" whose duties included farm financing and accounts management. The content stressed individualism and self-reliance associated with farming.

25. "A Few Profitable Common Things," *The Farmer's Wife,* July 1914, 64; Alta Lawson Littell, "Another Melissa Story: This Time, a Little Account Book Was the Bludgeon that Changed Dan's Mind," *The Farmer's Wife,* October 1920, 132.

26. "The Census Ceases to Be Absurd," *The Farmer's Wife,* February 1930, 3.

In *The Farmer's Wife*, content steadily depicted women as wives, mothers, homemakers, citizens, and businesswomen, not necessarily in that order. A regular feature was "They Had an Idea: And They Turned It into Money." Articles focused on farm women who had come up with innovative ways to make money through entrepreneurship on farms. Ideas included inviting city children to camp on the farm; raising and selling produce, such as strawberries and apples; selling Sunday dinner to city people looking for "real" food; making and selling fruit preserves; boarding city guests for summer vacations; raising and selling poultry; and making crafts that could be sold to raise money. Most discussions of farm women during this period stressed their roles as smart, capable, and innovative entrepreneurs who could stretch the boundaries of their traditional roles and, by doing so, add income to the farm business (and family).

Articles studied in 1940 issues of *Farm Journal* also discussed problems faced by farm women within a patriarchal structure. One reader's letter in 1940 sparked a discussion about who controlled the money on family farms—the men or the women. The responses, crafted by Carroll P. Streeter into an article in the April 1940 edition of the magazine, suggested that many farm families controlled money jointly, sometimes after serious struggles. In some farm families, women controlled the finances; in others, men did. When men controlled the finances, women either were given an allowance or had to account for every penny they needed for farm expenses, a situation described as humiliating. "Some [men] feel that part of the husband's job of cherishing and protecting a wife is to dole out money in a paternal manner," Streeter wrote. "Some are just selfish." Many writers described their strategies to make men see the necessity of joint control of finances, and others urged young couples to discuss money matters before they married. "It has to be settled eventually, and the earlier the better, they say." Regardless of how the money situation was settled, Streeter wrote, confidence and trust between husband and wife were common to all successful plans. "When the two partners have that attitude they not only work out the money problem but find most of the other answers to happy family life."[27]

Suffrage, Citizenship, and the Farm Woman

In 1915, suffrage was discussed in the issues of *Farm Journal* studied as a practical solution to women's problems. Women were claiming the

27. Streeter, "Who's the Banker at Your House?" *Farm Journal* 64:4 (April 1940): 43, 62ff.

vote as a right due them, with the full support of the farming community and national leaders. A short item written by W. J. Bryan in February 1915 argues that women should get the vote because most women, being intelligent and moral, were better fitted to vote than some men. "In every community where suffrage is an issue, every man who is living by crime and vice is against woman suffrage. These bad men know by instinct that woman is their enemy. Why don't good people all know that woman is their friend?"[28] An editor in August 1915 called for opinions on the subject: "Send in your vote on woman suffrage. Are you in favor or opposed? Women, criminals, idiots and crazy people alike are denied the ballot in most of the states. The question is, Ought women be taken out of that list or not?" The results of the poll were twenty to one in favor of suffrage.[29] Another article printed in the same issue was extracted from Beatrice Hale's book *What Women Want,* as particularly relevant to the problems of farm women: "If the farmer's children were economic assets to him, his wife was more so," Hale wrote, before listing, in detail, the kinds of work required of farm women. She concluded that farm women died young, while farm men married more than once and lived to a ripe old age.[30]

Hale's scathing commentary, an early feminist work, counters the construction of farm women as central to the tasks of running the farm. Farm women, Hale says, were worn out by the labor required of them. It seems notable that Hale's remarks were published in *Farm Journal,* and thus to a broad audience of farmers, both men and women. The farming community could have been aware of her book, and *Farm Journal* editors may have wanted to bring her views forward for discussion and, perhaps, to provoke change.

Farm women's participation in civic work was also stressed in issues of *The Farmer's Wife.* Farm women were discussed as active in the Women's Christian Temperance Union, the National Conservation Congress, and the International Congress of Farm Women. The editors, noting that farm women participated in these large organizations and in smaller ones closer to home, said farm women had not received the kind of press attention they deserved:

28. Bryan, "The Mother Argument," *Farm Journal* 39:2 (February 1915): 129.

29. *Farm Journal* 39:8 (August 1915): 442; "What They Say," *Farm Journal* 39:8 (August 1915): 429.

30. Hale, "The Good Old Times," from *What Women Want* (1914), reprinted in *Farm Journal* 39:8 (August 1915): 428.

> Rural press work is to be recognized as a factor in this great move of general interest to farm women and it is to be hoped that, dating from this meeting [of the International Congress of Farm Women], the home department of every rural paper in the country will do as much for women on the farm as men have done for men on the farm. *The Farmer's Wife,* uniquely standing as the only paper in this country published specifically for farm women, looks for greater developments along these lines than the press of the country has ever before attained.[31]

Some articles noted the role women played in their local communities, bringing people together to combat isolation and boredom as well as to provide services to others. Several articles discussed farm women's charitable work raising funds for schools and rest facilities, and others detailed the work of rural women's clubs. "It is the frank claim of those who belong to them, and the common observation of outsiders, that standards of thought, of living, of talk, and of social activity among rural women have been lifted to a higher plane by the Grange and similar organizations," Jennie Buelle of Ann Arbor, Michigan, told the International Congress of Farm Women in a speech in October 1911.[32]

Positions on suffrage and farm women were less clear than were positions on other issues in *The Farmer's Wife* content, and inherent tensions regarding the movement changed over time to reflect how farm women could use the vote. The editors of *The Farmer's Wife* included news about woman suffrage from the first issue studied during this time, but the topic was discussed cautiously. As women received the right to vote in separate states, the news was reported in the magazine. When the amendment for woman suffrage passed Congress, the magazine noted the importance of the event, and "News from Washington" began as a regular feature.

Before women received the vote, editors' comments and coverage of the suffrage movements around the world, on the whole, characterized suffrage as a good opportunity for women. Mary A. Whedon wrote about the annual convention of the National Suffrage Association in February 1912: "We have come back more determined to give ourselves

31. "The International Congress of Farm Women," *The Farmer's Wife,* October 1911, 142.

32. "Granges and Farmers' Clubs: What They Have Done for Farm Women," excerpts from a paper read by Buell to the International Congress of Farm Women in October 1911, reprinted in *The Farmer's Wife,* August 1912, 85.

more unreservedly to this important work." Whedon told her readers, "We hold that woman constitutes half the people and that sex should play no part in human activities, that the interests of man and woman are identical, that every human being must work out his salvation in world-building as well as in the individual soul-building."[33] Yet there was a tension, too, in characterizing the more militant members of the movement. In May 1912, the editors discussed their amazement at the activities of English suffragists, who were using civil disobedience to battle for the right to vote. Some had been jailed, deprived of food, and otherwise harassed for their part in public demonstrations for suffrage. "While we, in this country," the editors wrote, "see no ground for such militant methods nor any justice in such breaking of the laws, we cannot deny that the English women see it, or think they see it for themselves, when they will willingly suffer voluntary imprisonment, starvation and risk of life in fighting this battle of rights for their posterity."[34]

When Wisconsin farmers passed a resolution against woman suffrage, a scathing editorial denounced the action. "The Wisconsin farmer's wife is given the privilege to cook meals for her lord and master but cannot lift her voice to improve the laws of making and branding that food pure." Three paragraphs later, after discussing consumer law, education, and temperance as issues about which a woman should have a voice but could not, the editorial concludes: "This aforesaid lord and master is willing she should work days and care for the children nights (while he gets his full sleep) to aid in earning money to pay taxes, but that she should say how those taxes should be directed, taking a few minutes or a few hours to go with him to express her opinions, lo, THAT would be—well, you tell what."[35]

Suffrage moved to the background during 1914–1919, due perhaps to the threat of World War I. Farm women, nonetheless, were discussed as vital members of a larger civic community, capable of preserving food and doing the civic work that supported the troops and the home during times of war. Romantic fiction also appeared in the issues read. Tips on how to grow victory gardens or to use potatoes as laundry starch and advice on other thrifty measures dominated both articles

33. Whedon, "Work among Rural Clubs: Annual Convention of National Suffrage Ass'n," *The Farmer's Wife,* February 1912, 273.

34. "Militant Suffrage," *The Farmer's Wife,* May 1912, 372.

35. "Wisconsin's Antediluvian Farmers," *The Farmer's Wife,* August 1912, 86.

and the letters to the Home Club. "Now Is the Hour When No Woman Lives unto Herself—the Cause of One Is the Cause of All," one article proclaimed in November 1918, touting direct war aid through area Red Cross units staffed by farm women. Another article brought a message from the U.S. Food Administration (USFA) via author Ruth E. Morrison in March 1919. Quoting the administration, Morrison wrote that the USFA expected farm women to be vital to stemming the famine in Europe: "We look to the farm women to be guardians of the producing fields which come under their immediate supervision."[36]

The subject of politics also appeared in editorials in *The Farmer's Wife* that discussed the distribution of Smith-Lever funds to farm women and men as a marvelous step forward for farm women. Articles applauded women's gains. Some articles featured women county agents as home demonstrators for the techniques discussed during a period when technology in the preservation of food was rapidly changing. "She is striving to prove the dollars-and-cents value as well as the educational and health value of supplying the proper foods on the farm table," one article said of the woman county agent. "Clearly the woman county agent has come to stay. In the North and West, fourteen are now at work."[37]

The July 1919 editorial page lauded the Senate's passage of the suffrage bill. "Equal suffrage is born of the human sense of justice," the editors said. "Most women and some men believe that it will prove a friend indeed. Let us watch and wait. Incidentally, let us all vote whenever we can! Like the proverbial smile, 'It won't hurt much.'" The "News from Washington" column instituted in August 1919 featured legislative and national news of interest to farm women, who now would be voting on those issues. In April 1920, the editors again expressed appreciation for the suffrage movement and for woman suffrage when the Nineteenth Amendment was ratified: "Thus we see the final result of a struggle starting in the days of the Revolution and lasting for nearly one hundred and fifty years, truly a notable tribute to the quality of persistency."[38]

After ratification of the Nineteenth Amendment, women's citizenship was discussed seriously by both the editors and the letter writers to *The*

36. Morrison, "Our Daily Bread: A Message Direct from the United States Food Administration to Farm Women," *The Farmer's Wife*, March 1919, 231.

37. "With the Woman County Agents: These Home Demonstrators Bring Practical Scientific Knowledge to the Farm Woman's Door," *The Farmer's Wife*, December 1916, 144.

38. "The Granting of Suffrage," *The Farmer's Wife*, April 1920, 356.

Farmer's Wife. National news of interest continued to be directed to farm women, and articles regarding the importance of farm women's work and their vital role on farms and in the community persisted. A series of columns in 1922 discussed citizenship as a collection of obligations and responsibilities now thrust upon farm women, suggesting that farm women needed education about their new rights and responsibilities. "Curiously, the success of our system of government depends upon our *voluntary* action. Voting is the most that the vast majority of us can do and the least any of us should do for our country," Ellis Meredith wrote in June 1922. In another article, he discussed the different political parties, platforms, and tickets from which women could choose in casting their vote. "Try to hear all the county candidates and as many as possible of those running for the higher offices. If you wish to be an intelligent voter, hear both sides—*and keep your temper,*" Meredith advised.[39]

The political discussion in *The Farmer's Wife* abruptly ended in 1923, possibly due to a change in editorial policy. The magazine continued to be staffed and edited by women, but in April 1923 the male publisher of the journal announced an editorial change to "better serve" the readers. This change appeared to be aimed at better serving the domestic sphere. Depictions of farm women as important and as businesswomen continued in addition to depictions of the farm woman's role as a mother and homemaker. A regular feature in the early years concerned the roles of farm women as mothers, but features devoted to children's health and well-being became more frequent and dominated the magazine pages from 1923 to 1930.

More attention was paid to farm women's roles in politics and activism in 1925 issues of the *Country Gentleman* studied than in earlier issues. Mary Sherman, president of the National Federation of Women's Clubs, contributed articles on women's roles in global politics and farm women's concerns in politics. "Women, organized, marching together, thinking sanely, working steadily—it is up to us to demand, to get, to maintain world peace," she asserted in an article published on the Fourth of July in 1925. In another article, Sherman noted that she had been born on a farm in New York State and lived and worked there until she was ten

39. Meredith, "The Woman Citizen's Job: A Brief Outline of Her New Rights, Duties and Privileges," *The Farmer's Wife,* June 1922, 13 (emphasis in original); "For Women Voters: Information as to Tickets: Straight, Diluted and Mixed," *The Farmer's Wife,* September 1922, 110 (emphasis in original).

years old. "Perhaps it is those years that make me feel that the farm women can bring into our club life some of the vital elements, the salty savor that it now lacks. If we could count upon her assistance, upon her interest and her cooperation, I believe there is nothing that we could not undertake successfully," she wrote, stressing her view that farm women were needed in women's national concerns and programs.[40]

In 1925 issues of the *Farm Journal* studied, fewer features than in earlier years addressed farm methods and progress and more concerned business and government actions and policies that were affecting farmers. Readers discussed the importance of self-reliance and individualism in ways that evoked the agrarian republican tradition espoused by Thomas Jefferson. This editorial, for example, relates individualism and farm culture:

> The trouble with these Congressmen, and with many other people, too, is that they do not think of farmers as human beings, but as a huge mass, wholly apart from the rest of the population, and prone to chin whiskers and a perpetual grouch.
>
> The truth is that most farmers do know exactly what they want, but not all farmers want the same thing or things. On the contrary, farm people will be found arrayed on both sides of almost any question of legislation or economics. There are almost as many conflicts of interest between different groups of farmers as there are between farmers and city people.[41]

A stress on the value of individualism over collective action was seen multiple times in successive issues of *Farm Journal*. Farming, it seems, was viewed as a treasured source of employment that allowed people an independence to stand or fall on their own efforts.

In the 1930 issues of the *Farm Journal* read, features offered practical farming advice from farmers, as opposed to advice from government or academic experts. Quoting from an 1880 issue of the *Farm Journal*, the editors in 1930 reinforced their policy of stressing commonsense farming by having farmers share ideas and advice: "We have no great professors writing for the *Farm Journal*. None of our guns are big guns. Most of those who contribute are working farmers and busy housewives,

40. Sherman, "Women's Crusade for Peace," *Country Gentleman* 90:27 (July 4, 1925): 26; "Farm Women and the Federation," *Country Gentleman* 90:16 (April 18, 1925): 19.

41. "Farmers Want What They Want, But What?" *Farm Journal* 49:11 (November 1925): 12.

who write with their sleeves rolled up. Our plan may be all wrong, but it enables us to get out a paper that the practical farmer likes."[42] The writers of this statement treat men and women as equally important contributors of knowledge about farming.

Despite any views of particular editorial staff to the contrary, the *Country Gentleman*'s content emphasized the centrality of farm women to the farm business, and more discussion of farm women as citizens was seen in the 1940 issues than in earlier ones studied. The *Country Gentlewoman* in October 1940, for example, focused on educating farm women about government and civics to help those interested in participating in politics. "Women of the rural communities, particularly, have been doing much quiet and effective thinking. And, surely, no group is equipped to make better use of the privilege of citizenship," wrote Helen Randolph Churchill. She continued:

> Women whose problems are practical ones concerned with the seasons, with growing things, with feeding the world; women whose minds are not cluttered with inconsequential, artificially stimulated interests, are prone to think calmly, carefully, and are bound to evolve sound conclusions. It is no accident that shrewd politicians of all parties, when they would a-wooing go, seek first the farmer. They well know that his propensity for independent thinking is a force to be reckoned with. In times such as are presaged by present conditions, the farmer and his wife may prove to be the bulwark of our liberties.[43]

This suggestion that farmers were better fitted for citizenship and political participation than were their city counterparts was seen also in farm women's writings in mainstream magazines, and it is part of the dominant construction of farm women as central to the farm business, home, and community. It is also part of the construction of farm women as wise, practical, and plainspoken that was seen in the mainstream magazines.

Urban versus Rural Life

Concern over the flight of men and women to the city was seen in the 1910 issues of *Farm Journal* studied. Editorials discussed how to keep farm youth from leaving, for example. Articles showed that advice from

42. "50 Years Ago," *Farm Journal* 54:3 (March 1930): 12.
43. Churchill, "Open Season for Politics," *Country Gentleman* 110:10 (October 1940): 39.

farm women was respected within this culture. For example, "Feminine Dairy Wisdom," a regular feature written by Dorothy Tucker, who had also been a regular contributor to *Country Gentleman,* gave advice on raising cows for milk. Other regular features, many with women's bylines, offered advice about raising poultry and growing produce for sale. Editorials said girls should receive a solid education and the same training in job skills accorded to boys. "Every girl should be able to earn as good a living as her brother, and, moreover, should rejoice in her ability to do so," said one editorial.[44] Another editorial argued that this was practical because families who wanted to keep the boys on the farm must attract the girls to farm life. P. E. Clement wrote:

> Visit school some day—you don't go half as often as you ought—and see if it is any wonder that your girl is not interested in helping mother as she used to be, when all about her the idea is prevalent that she must get an education to escape the life of a drudge—that is, of a housewife. Then take a look around the kitchen. Maybe a few dollars invested in new and labor-saving machinery would add wonderfully to its interest for both mother and daughter. Educate the girl to be womanly and to appreciate feminine things. Teach her the value and beauty of farm life, and she will be proud to be a farmer lady. When the girls want to live on the farm, much will have been done toward keeping the boys there.[45]

Despite the patriarchal subtext of the passage, a belief in the importance of women to the business of farming is apparent.

Mary Sherman, president of the National Federation of Women's Clubs, explained in 1925 that farm women believed themselves to be set apart from city women. She recounted what she called an "unusual" experience of being invited to a rural women's club meeting, and she emphasized how much she enjoyed being there. Her hostess's remark, at the end of the meeting, that she felt Sherman to be "one of us" led Sherman to comment: "And I am one of every little rural organization in America, whether it is a federated club or not, because I feel I belong there. I want them all to come into my big family."[46]

The distinction between the city and country culture also was alluded to in other magazine content that bemoaned the loss of farm sons and daughters to the city and pitied city couples who failed to have children

44. "Household," *Farm Journal* 34:12 (December 1910): 619.
45. Clement, "Keep the Girls on the Farm," *Farm Journal* 34:9 (September 1910): 456.
46. Sherman, "Farm Women and the Federation," 22.

due to economic circumstances. "There is something about the city that is blighting to that kind of life. It is restless, filled with uncertainties and dreads," one editorial said in July 1925, after having commented on recent research that suggested farm families were having more children than city families. The editorial lamented the inadequacy of family life in the city. "In the balance sheet of advantages, all those the city can offer do not offset this one item in favor of country life. For there is nothing that counts so much in the aggregate of human happiness as the love of a child, no tragedy so pitiful as the home denied it."[47] This suggests that at least one editorial writer considered children more than a simple investment to assure labor in the farming community. It is not surprising that the same writer showed a strong anti-city bias, because the *Country Gentleman* acted as a farm booster.

The 1930 issues of *Country Gentleman* made clear the magazine's role as a farm booster. Some items lamented conditions in the cities that were hardest hit by the stock market crash in 1929 while claiming farm life as immune to its effects. An August 1930 editorial cartoon by C. H. Sykes shows "The Farmer's Bread Line." A smiling farm woman calls happy field workers to dinner as children play nearby.[48] Some content overtly and implicitly suggested that city workers could have avoided the hardships they were enduring if they had stayed on the farm. Editorials also reinforced the notion that city life had led to chaos, instability, and loss of pride and serenity. One such editorial addressed the decline in the consumption of corn bread, with accompanying angst:

> But corn bread is far more than a food. It's a form of art, a national expression. A crispy slice of corn bread, piping hot and properly lubricated with yellow butter or creamy ham gravy, produces in one the same aesthetic delight, the same exaltation of spirit, as a lovely sonnet or a fine mural. Corn bread, like an after-dinner pipe or an open fire, helps to make a man tolerant of his fellows and philosophical about his own woes.
>
> That is why the retrogression of corn-bread eating can be looked upon only with the gravest apprehension. This pell-mell age needs philosophy; it needs the rich homely things of life. A man can't invite his own soul while nibbling a lettuce sandwich served to him across a marble-topped soda-fountain counter.[49]

47. "Country Children," *Country Gentleman* 90:28 (July 11, 1925): 18.
48. "The Farmer's Bread Line," *Country Gentleman* 95:8 (August 1930): 11.
49. "Corn Bread, a Form of Art," *Country Gentleman* 95:8 (August 1930): 20.

Such statements may epitomize farmers' reactions to years of enticements in mainstream publications about city life and the steady paychecks provided by industry. Farm-oriented writers seem to have been saying that city living drained the soul, and the economic conditions in the cities at the time simply proved the value of farm life. The theme was seen in articles under the "Country Gentlewoman" heading that discussed entertaining city friends on the farm. Mary Walker wrote in 1930 that the highway systems had not only brought the farm closer to the city; they had also brought the city closer to the farm. She suggested setting a regular time when farm women would receive their city friends and provided two rules: "do not ape your city friends" and "let simplicity be the keynote of any entertainment." She wrote of city visitors as having jaded appetites that could only be whetted by good, wholesome country cooking.[50]

The anti-city bias was seen again in issues from the *Country Gentleman* five years later. Despite the existence of harsh economic conditions everywhere during the period now known as the Great Depression, men and women farmers were portrayed positively in the 1935 issues of the magazine, which seems to have implied that farmers, as "landed gentry" of the United States, lived rich lives. This notion, in stark contrast to stories shared in other media, seems to suggest that only those living in the cities were victims of the Depression.

To be sure, articles in the *Country Gentleman* provided advice on economical means of producing food and clothing on the farm, but the level of farm boosterism seems anachronistic, considering the conditions reported elsewhere. Certainly the contrast between the Dorothea Lange photograph reproduced in the Introduction and the illustrations here is stark. Moreover, due to changes in the magazine's structure, content by and about women outweighed all other content. Romantic fiction, fashion, homemaking tips, recipes, and the usual business tips for women pervaded articles focused on the farm home. Women's accomplishments and achievements—not limited to those of farm women—were featured in regular articles by Genevieve Forbes Herrick. Illustrations for *Country Gentlewoman,* bound under separate cover in the back of the magazine, showed healthy, pink-cheeked women, smartly dressed and engaged in such country leisure activities as golf.

Despite the boosterism for farm women, country living, and business, the magazine's editorials warned against New Deal measures. One such editorial denounced the idea that surplus commodities existed:

50. Walker, "Entertaining City Friends," *Country Gentleman* 95:8 (August 1930): 54.

> For example, the statement that "stomachs are not expansive" is utterly meaningless, when perhaps two-thirds of the stomachs of the nation have never been properly filled. We say there is too much cotton, but people are going ragged. There is no doubt that many things are wrong, but the idea that we have too much of almost any commodity is silly; it will not stand analysis. And most of the remedies proposed to cure our ills are equally silly.[51]

Others argued against the casual moving of people from industrialized cities to worn-out farmland in an effort to combat the economic effects of the depression. One editorial about the trends in shifting population, said, in part:

> People ought not to be moved about casually, onto small acreages here and off large blocks of condemned land there, without the full consequences being taken into consideration. There has been enough of this difficult human reassorting already without any more being deliberately added.
>
> One thing the social planners do not know is that it takes a lot of special knowledge, skill and work to get a living out of a plot of ground.[52]

Here, the failures of many such displaced families to earn a living from their land seem to be blamed on social planners' lack of knowledge about farming demands.

The 1935 issues of *Farm Journal* studied emphasized women as central to farm business and farm life, as seen earlier. Classified ads offered stock for sale, and larger ads offered labor-saving devices as money savers, too. Women's bylines continued to appear in the journal. Commentary focused on drought conditions, crop conditions, and economic factors that were dragging many farmers into financial ruin. The shared tips among farmers located throughout the journal suggest that some were managing to succeed despite hardships brought by weather and economic problems to their way of life.

Farmers had been hit hard by the depression, but complaints were rare to nonexistent and only optimistic viewpoints and suggestions of practical help were seen in the 1935 issues of the *Farm Journal* studied. The first editorial of January 1935 asked, "What's 'A Good Living and 10%'? It is a phrase invented by this magazine to express our idea of what every capable farmer is entitled to receive, in an average year, for

51. "Research Needed," *Country Gentleman* 105:3 (March 1935): 20.
52. "Tragedy of the Movers," *Country Gentleman* 105:6 (June 1935): 20.

his labors. It is an ideal, or a standard, or measuring stick, or whatever figure suits you best."[53] This emphasis on the idea that farming can and should be profitable, even this far into the depression-ridden thirties, suggests that the editors had not given up on the farming industry despite conditions that made farming difficult.

This optimism and a respect for individual farming practices were seen in anti–New Deal, anti–Franklin Delano Roosevelt articles. Editorials called for the end of the National Recovery Administration (NRA), an office—ruled unconstitutional in 1935—that directed big businesses to cut labor hours, raise wages, and regulate competition. Editors called the NRA "a total flop" that had "injured agriculture."[54] An item on the same editorial page called on farmers to reduce production, saying consumers were unable to buy the surpluses being generated by some farms:

> The hungry should be fed, the ill-clothed kept warm. But that is not the responsibility of agriculture, except as it may be the duty of individual farmers in individual cases. It is the responsibility of the nation as a whole, and more especially the industries and trades and their social agencies.
>
> Agriculture is the [scape]goat for many things. It should not be made the [scape]goat for maladjustments to the rest of the social structure, which it can do nothing to correct, and for which it can not possibly be blamed.[55]

The October issue in 1935 included the Bill of Rights in its entirety, with this comment: "At a time when a centralized government is showing itself more than willing to usurp control of local affairs, and to curtail the freedom and security of the citizen by fair means or foul, it seems worth while to reprint above the ten Amendments that made this nation possible, and which have kept it a fit place for a free people to live."[56] The emphasis here on individualism, freedom, and the idea that freedom should be defined as freedom from government interference in local affairs seems a liberal stance in a magazine that opposed New Deal programs.

By 1940, changes in the format of the *Country Gentleman* made it easier to locate editorial columns and readers' letters. Articles were again seen that treated farming as the best way of life in the United States and

53. "A Good Living *and* 10%," *Farm Journal* 59:1 (January 1935): 3.
54. "End the NRA," *Farm Journal*, 59:4 (April 1935): 6.
55. "'Over-Production,'" *Farm Journal* 59:4 (April 1935): 6.
56. "Liberty and Security of the Citizen," *Farm Journal* 59:10 (October 1935): 6.

that treated women as central to that way of life. The individual boys' and girls' columns found in issues of previous years were replaced with "Modern Juniors," a column devoted to young farm people that often featured 4-H activities. The *Country Gentlewoman* again was a significant portion of the magazine issues studied, and it focused on helping farm women succeed as homemakers. The magazine aimed to draw the entire farm family as an audience, and its articles treated the farm family as the core of the farming business. However, a subtle shift was seen in 1940 issues in that, while women were treated as being at the enter of the farming business, their own, personal, entrepreneurial interests were downplayed in the pages specifically directed toward them. Editorials seem to have been more expressive in 1940 than in earlier years about farm women's roles in the farm home. One editorial decried the use of whipped cream with pancakes. "We hope someone brings this bit of treachery to the attention of the Dies Committee, which is investigating un-American activities," said the writer, concluding with memories of pancake night on the farm, when the family moved to the kitchen and pancakes "flew" from stove to plates. "Dad and the boys always tagged an eating marathon, and it was a puny lad who stopped at less than a dozen. Naturally, you permit no tampering with memories like these. Whipped cream on pancakes! Where does the New York editor expect us to eat such a sissy concoction—in a boudoir? Sometimes we envy Hitler his concentration camps."[57] This editorial expresses a strong need to retain past traditions and blames the city editor for this loss. The anti-city bias seems to have dominated after Philip S. Rose took over as editor in 1930. In this editorial city life is depicted as violating treasured memories in which the farm woman waited on her men hand-and-foot from the kitchen, arguing against change for successful farmers.

The *Country Gentleman* was under new editorship in 1945. The issues studied reinforced the idea that all aspects of the farming business converged through the farm home. The farm also was depicted as a haven in an unsafe world, and the farm family as the strongest support system available for soldiers returning from World War II battlefields. Some articles emphasized jobs for veterans in rural areas, and some focused on the great green spaces that soothed the saddened spirits of those

57. "Pancakes for Supper," *Country Gentleman* 110:1 (January 1940): 18. The true horrors of the concentration camps may not have been known at the time of this editorial's publication.

who had served overseas. Editorials discussed the policies and conditions of a postwar United States in troubled tones. Concern about farm tenancy, the lifting of restrictions on gasoline sales and motorcar travel, and national agricultural policies dominated editorial pages that consistently advocated less government spending and more restrictions of city encroachment on farmland and communities. However, editorials cautiously supported certain government actions, such as price controls. "Price controls are irritating and are not a normal part of our way of living. But those left should be kept in effect until adequate production and competition remove the dangers of a runaway price rise," one editorial said in November 1945.[58] Additionally, editors cautioned farmers to be wary of purchasing leftover war surplus equipment, particularly items that needed to be remodeled for use on farms.

The *Country Gentlewoman,* at this point officially labeled a "magazine within a magazine," included fashion, crafts, recipes, and household tips. Other content, by contrast, rarely addressed women's issues and instead focused nearly exclusively on politics and farm progress tips that presumably were of interest to women as well as to men. Featured content was aimed at the total farm family, and the family farm was depicted as a site of peace. Letters to the editors, a regular feature in 1945 issues studied, carried signatures of both men and women, who expressed a variety of opinions on the politics of the day.

The centrality of farming to global politics and interests was stressed in both *Farm Journal* and *The Farmer's Wife* in 1950 issues studied. Discussions focused on crop pricing and alternate farming methods in both. One such article, in November 1950, discussed what the family should do if an A-bomb fell near the farm. Families could take refuge in the fruit cellar, which, if made of reinforced concrete, should provide protection from the blast, heat, and radioactivity. "Fireproof" housekeeping was stressed as "all-important" to keep the blast's heat from sparking fires in flammable materials in the home. "All in all, there is no reason for believing that the use of nuclear weapons—even those of improved design—necessarily means the end of all life on earth," Richard Gerstell wrote. "Nevertheless, unless we maintain peace, those weapons will surely bring death and destruction on a scale now scarcely imaginable."[59]

58. "Price Controls and the Farmer," *Country Gentleman* 115:11 (November 1945): 124.

59. Gerstell, "If an A-Bomb Fell Near Your Farm," *Farm Journal* 74:11 (November 1950): 32–33, 83ff.

The article downplayed the potential effects but discussed farm women as having an active role in protecting the family—through preservation of food and housekeeping. Farm women's roles in the atomic age thus were given new importance. Nonetheless, 1955 and 1960 features constructed farm women as homemakers rather than businesswomen, despite continued emphasis on their roles as farm managers.

The *Farm Journal* issues read portrayed farmers as ideologically conservative, individualistic, and patriotic, and this portrayal seemed stronger in 1950 issues than in earlier ones. A February 1950 editorial about President Harry S. Truman's State of the Union Address said several proposals infringed upon individual freedom. "Millions of people share the illusion that government can, by passing laws, accomplish results which are beyond the powers of any government to accomplish," the editorial contended. It continued:

> Many Republicans, many Democrats, share this dangerous illusion. Politicians especially tend to promote it, because the more they can promise, the more votes they hope to get.
>
> President Truman believes this illusion. He does not intend to be an enemy of freedom. Nevertheless his state-of-the-union message contained at least a dozen proposals that encroach upon individual freedom.[60]

Other editorials made the same points, regardless of the overall topic. Government always will try to extend its power, and Americans must continue to work hard to keep their individual freedoms, the editors argued. "Americans will work harder to win whatever struggle is ahead if they are told the truth, if they are left free to express their judgments, and are allowed to work without shackles," said an August 1950 editorial, ostensibly about the fighting in Korea. "The great task for farmers, as for all Americans, will be to keep whole both the U.S.A. and American freedom. Freedom is our greatest resource, and our most powerful weapon."[61] A 1955 editorial suggested that Russians could produce more food if they were free to do so. The editors called freedom "the best fertilizer for production." A September 1960 editorial said, "As farmer citizens of this wonderful America, our first obligation is to make sure that human liberty endures for ourselves."[62]

60. "How to Strike a Blow," *Farm Journal* 74:2 (February 1950): 12.
61. "The Strongest Weapon," *Farm Journal* 74:8 (August 1950): 8.
62. "Come, and Bring Your Wives," *Farm Journal* 79:4 (April 1955): 190; "As Citizens and Farmers," *Farm Journal* 84:9 (September 1960): 122.

Content in each of the three farming magazines uniformly portrayed farm women as central to the farm home and business, as respected members of a larger farming community, and as successful farmers and entrepreneurs in their own rights. Content also depicted a rift between farm and city dwellers that grew over time and was most apparent in times of crisis. The role of farming in a larger political and civic arena was expressed as of paramount importance, despite dwindling numbers of farm dwellers, and the philosophy surrounding discussions of farming and politics was one of self-reliance, individualism, and patriotism.

In the *Farm Journal* and *The Farmer's Wife,* letters to the editor were routinely published for the whole of the fifty-year period studied. Those letters ultimately reveal much about farm women's roles during this important era and provide insight into what farm women may have thought about myriad issues. Their letters, along with journalistic writings by other farm women, will be considered next.

5

For Farm Women "The Only Class of Workers Who Are Absolutely without Representation"

"Women can no longer hide behind their husbands and fathers and brothers by saying, 'I don't pay any attention to politics. That is the men's business,'" Laura Ingalls Wilder told her *Missouri Ruralist* readers in 1919. "Nor can they safely vote as their men folks do without any other reason for so doing. We women know in our hearts, tho we would not admit it, that our men are not infallible. They do sometimes make mistakes and have the wrong ideas. Frankly now, is it not true? This being the case, now that the responsibility is ours, we shall be obliged to think things out for ourselves if we are honest and fair to them and ourselves."[1]

Wilder was one of a number of farm women who wrote as journalists and as freelance contributors to national magazines and local rural newspapers, using their writing talent to secure additional income for the farm family and thus illustrating the entrepreneurial skills discussed in previous chapters. Many farm women used journalism to make money, but many more wrote to the letters columns, particularly in *The Farmer's Wife,* to connect with other farm women. Their expressions there suggest a sense of community formed through the medium of a national magazine, a suggestion borne out by the responses I received from farm women to my simple request for their stories published in a contemporary magazine.

The significance of farm women's ideas regarding their roles, particularly in the larger global arena, lies in understanding that these women raised at least two generations of young people, many of whom emigrated to the city. The ways in which these young people were taught about women's roles, citizenship, and political philosophy is directly relevant to the actions of these generations. The "Country Contributor,"

1. Laura Ingalls Wilder, "Women's Duty at the Polls," *Ruralist,* April 20, 1919, in Stephen W. Hines, ed., *Laura Ingalls Wilder, Farm Journalist: Writings from the Ozarks,* 182.

for example, wrote in a July 1910 *Ladies' Home Journal* column that mothers were responsible for teaching their children such enduring values as patriotism: "Your conception of patriotism, then, will probably be your boy's conception of it when he grows to be a man—at least, if you take the trouble to tell him about it in an interesting way."[2]

Given that influence, an understanding of farm women's ideas about patriotism, citizenship, and other such concepts provides clues to how such influence might have manifested. For example, the concept of self-reliance was significant to many of the farm women who wrote to the publications studied. As the "Country Contributor" wrote, farm women's worthiness to be citizens lay in their self-reliance, defined in this case as the ability and willingness to physically fight as necessary for one's country: "Though I have never clamored for the ballot, and do not know just what I would do with it if I had it, I fancy I am a little nearer to the qualification which Mrs. Humphrey Ward says women lack than most of my sex. I am not afraid of a gun, and I used to know how to load and shoot one after a fashion."[3]

The names of some of the writers considered in this chapter may be familiar, and it must be stressed that the primary sources used for this research were not systematically selected and are not representative or inclusive of all such sources that may exist. However, taken together, these sources reveal the voices of some farm women and are valuable for that alone.

The Importance of Farm Women

One farm woman, Laura Ingalls Wilder, is known for her fictional series of children's books, but she was a regular contributor to the *Missouri Ruralist,* her local farm newspaper, before writing those books. Wilder, born in 1867, and her husband, Almanzo, ran Rocky Ridge Farm in Mansfield, Missouri, from 1894 until Almanzo's death in 1949. Wilder remained at Rocky Ridge Farm until her death in 1957. From 1911 to 1926, Wilder used her writing to supplement her farm income, encouraged by both her editor at the *Ruralist* and her daughter, Rose Wilder Lane. Her first fiction book, *Little House in the Big Woods,* was published in 1932, with seven books following. The last of her books,

2. "The Ideas of a Plain Country Woman," *Ladies' Home Journal,* July 1910, 20.
3. Ibid.

These Happy Golden Years, was published in 1943. Other writings from Wilder's desk have since been posthumously published, and her heirs have continued to build on Wilder's fame through a television show and several new series of books based on the lives of other women in her family. Wilder's columns for the *Ruralist,* which have since been republished in *Laura Ingalls Wilder, Farm Journalist,* focus on the themes of working conditions, socialization, self-improvement, and redefining women's work. Each theme is discussed in turn below.

An old adage that appears several times in Wilder's discussions of farmwork is: "Farmer works from sun to sun, but woman's work is never done." On the farm, Wilder cared for her house and garden and often worked as the only "hired hand." Her columns depict farmwork as unrelenting and unceasing.

Wilder wrote in 1913 about farm women: "Thinking persons realize that the woman, on the farm, is a most important factor in the success or failure of the whole farm business and that, aside from any kindly feeling toward her, it pays in dollars and cents to conserve her health and strength." She added, "Women on the farm have not as a rule the conveniences that city housekeepers have and their work includes much outside work, such as gardening, caring for chickens and gathering as well as putting up fruits and vegetables."[4] Women's work also included going to the spring to haul water into the home, sawing wood as necessary, and caring for animals in place of the veterinarian on occasion. For Wilder, farmwork also involved keeping farm accounts, helping run farm machinery at harvest time, and filling in for Almanzo, her husband, when his health didn't allow him to complete his work.[5]

Wilder's writing made clear a need for help in the farm kitchen, and she was thankful for any kind of conveniences that money or ingenuity could provide. For example, she praised the gas generator in one of her first articles for the *Ruralist.* "Bless it! Besides doing the work of a hired man outside, it can be made to do the pumping of the water and the churning, turn the washing machine and even run the sewing machine." "Favors the Small Farm Home," printed in February 1911, advocates the ideal home as one made by a man and woman together, and it

4. Wilder, "Shorter Hours for Farm Women," *Ruralist,* June 28, 1913, in Hines, ed., *Farm Journalist,* 22–23.

5. Almanzo had suffered a stroke early in their marriage and thereafter had difficulty walking and performing some physical tasks.

outlines the many conveniences that make running a farm possible for just these two people.[6] In other columns, she passed on time- and work-saving tips, such as using carpet to cushion feet when pedaling a sewing machine and a fast way to make grape jelly. She also advocated strategies such as doing the major housework a little at a time all through the year, rather than all at once twice a year, as had been the tradition. Rather than doing every chore by one's self, Wilder advocated cutting out some of the traditional housework, such as ironing sheets and beating carpets. "Never do I have the house in a turmoil and myself exhausted as it used to be when I house-cleaned twice a year," she wrote. "The applied science of the elimination of work can best be studied by each housekeeper for herself, but believe me, it is well worth studying."[7]

A problem for her and other farm women was lack of available help for hire. In one column, Wilder wrote about the idlers who perpetually took up space in the town square, all of whom refused to work on a farm. "Who wants to work like a farmer anyway!" one exclaimed at the suggestion. Wilder wrote with a little sarcasm:

> No one seems to want to "work like a farmer," except the farmer's wife. Well! Perhaps she does not exactly want to, but from the way she goes about it no one would suspect that she did not. In our neighborhood we are taking over more of the chores to give the men longer days in the field. . . . Their hands are quite full now and it seems that about the only way they could procure more help would be to marry more wives.[8]

With her usual good humor, she added in a later column that no one should be denied the pleasure of working: "Man realized [the joy of working] soon after he was sentenced to 'earn his bread by the sweat of his brow,' and with his usual generosity he lost no time in letting his womenkind in on a good thing."[9]

Offering strategies for helping women with their work, Wilder advocated rest for dealing with the work that must be done. She urged readers to take a little time every day to completely relax both mind and body, as a friend of hers did. Such relaxation, she wrote, could renew

6. Wilder, "Favors the Small Farm Home," *Ruralist,* February 18, 1911, in Hines, ed., *Farm Journalist,* 14.

7. Wilder, "Join 'Don't Worry' Club," *Ruralist,* March 20, 1916, in ibid., 58–62.

8. Wilder, "Haying While the Sun Shines," *Ruralist,* July 20, 1916, in ibid., 76.

9. Wilder, "Work Makes Life Interesting," *Ruralist,* February 20, 1919, in ibid., 175.

strength and relieve the stress on women. "[I]f we allowed ourselves more idle time we would conserve our nervous strength and health to more than the value of the work we could accomplish by emulating at all times the little busy bee." In another column, she added to this line of thought: "Work is like other good things in that it should not be indulged in to excess, but a reasonable amount that is of value to one's self and to the world, as is any honest, well-directed labor, need never descend into drudgery."[10]

Wilder devoted a great deal of space to advising women about how to achieve personal goals. Education, she argued, should be stressed in the farm home and should include lifelong learning and self-improvement. Socializing with other farm women could provide some of that lifelong learning, she argued, and combat the isolation so many women felt on their farms. "Learning things is most fascinating and I think it adds joy to life to be continually learning things so that we may be able to go on with it creditably," she wrote in 1924.[11] Wilder seems to have so enjoyed learning new things—and socializing as she did so—that she helped to found a women's educational club called the Athenians, about which she wrote for her readers. Country women did not need to remain isolated on their farms, she argued; opportunities to socialize with other women could always be found or created. One such group simply got together with their crocheting once a month, taking turns playing host.

Wilder stressed the need for farm children to be educated. Because of the dearth of hired help, children on farms were made to work as hard as the adults, often at the sacrifice of their schooling. "All the instruction in the farm papers, the wealth of knowledge, of new ideas and methods, of mutual help and the getting together spirit that all good farm papers are working to spread, does not reach the farmers who cannot read an article in a paper and understand it," she lamented in 1919.[12] But the problem, as Wilder described it, was complicated by a number of factors. Put more money into schools, she said, and farm children will be required to work even longer hours to help their parents pay the extra taxes so that other children have the advantage of schooling. Wilder endorsed valuing education at home first:

10. Wilder, "Sometimes Misdirected Energy May Cease to Be a Virtue," *Ruralist,* February 20, 1916, in ibid., 52; "The Farm Home," *Ruralist,* August 20, 1920, in ibid., 230.

11. Wilder, "As a Farm Woman Thinks," *Ruralist,* April 1, 1924, in ibid., 308.

12. Wilder, "The Farm Home," *Ruralist,* May 5, 1919, in ibid., 183.

> We think we cannot afford to give the children the proper schooling, "besides, their help is needed on the farm," we say. We shall pay for that education which we do not give them. Oh! We shall pay for it! When we see our children inefficient and handicapped, perhaps thru life, for the lack of the knowledge they should have gained in their youth, we shall pay in our hurt pride and our regret that we did not give them a fair chance, if in no other way, tho quite likely we shall pay in money too. The children, more's the pity, must pay also.[13]

In one column, Wilder cited a poor farm couple, the Findleys, as examples. They placed their children's education above the family's immediate need for their services on the farm. Mrs. Findley took in extra washing to pay for schoolbooks and taught her children to read as soon as they were old enough. She told Wilder, "[I]f people say the Jess Findley family were poor, they'll say, too, that the children were well educated, for that is where we are putting our life's work—into their heads." Wilder said the Findleys were providing the best service they could to their children:

> When Mrs. Findley had finished her story I mentally took note of one thought which has escaped so many of us. It was not the old story of an education always being within the grasp of those who really seek it, but in raising the standard of the Findley home, the standard of four homes of the future had been elevated to the point which we like to think of as a representative "American Home."[14]

The point, Wilder stressed repeatedly, was that each person backslides without going forward and learning as much as possible. Self-improvement required continuing to strive to go forward. "If we do not strive to gain we lose what we already have, for just so surely as 'practice makes perfect,' the want of practice or the lack of exercise of talents and knowledge makes for the opposite condition."[15]

During the time Wilder wrote, the world was undergoing great changes. World War I, with accompanying issues of global concern, appears to have significantly affected how she thought and wrote about farmwork and farm lives during this period. Farm production assumed

13. Wilder, "To Buy or Not to Buy," *Ruralist,* September 20, 1917, in ibid., 123.

14. Wilder, "How the Findleys Invest Their Money," *Ruralist,* August 1, 1922, in ibid., 275.

15. Wilder, "Are You Going Ahead?" *Ruralist,* February 20, 1917, in ibid., 102–3.

greater importance for her than ever before. At the same time, Wilder said women seemed to have been left out of the organizing discussions that would help with food production on the farms, despite women's crucial roles there.

In July 1917, Wilder related a story about a meeting called by the Missouri State College of Agriculture to gather farm and town folks together to organize farmers' clubs for the war effort. "As I looked around at the people, I thought what a representative gathering it was," Wilder wrote. "Judging from the appearance of the crowd, the women were as much interested in the subject of food production as a means of national defense as the men were, for fully as many women as men were present and they were seemingly as eager to learn from the speaker anything that farmers could do to increase the food supply." A club was formed after the meeting, but women were not included in its organization. When they were invited to the first meeting as an afterthought, only two women showed up. "Quite likely it was the women's own fault and if they had taken part as a matter of course it would have been accepted as such, but it seems rather hard to do this unless we are shown the courtesy of being mentioned," Wilder wrote. But the incident seems to have grated on her, because her continued observations on the status of farm women were sharper than before. "What would happen to the 'increase of production' if the women did not cook for the harvest hands, to say nothing of taking care of the hired help the remainder of the year?" she asked. "Why shouldn't farm women's work be recognized by state authorities and others in other ways than urging her to more and yet more work when her working day is already somewhere from 14 to 16 hours long?"[16]

The value of women and their work on the farm, Wilder argued in countless ways over thirteen years, was immeasurable, and their worth should be recognized. Wilder pointed out that the woman's commission of the Council of National Defense was organizing in the cities to fight for an eight-hour day, living wages, and one day of rest per week, but farm women were left out of the discussion. "There is not yet, so far as I know, any committee to co-operate with the farm women in obtaining for them either an 8-hour day or a living profit and if they are denied an active part in the farmers' clubs they are the only class of workers who are absolutely without representation," Wilder pointed out.[17]

16. Wilder, "Without Representation," *Ruralist*, July 5, 1917, in ibid., 114–15.
17. Ibid., 115.

Many of her columns stress the importance of women's work on the farm, and she optimistically wrote of the equality women could achieve with their partners. Wilder repeatedly encouraged women to respect their own positions, stand up for themselves, and take their places on the farm. In 1922, she wrote of a lecture she had read about that portrayed the plight of America's farm women as pathetic:

> Now I don't want any tears shed over my position, but I've since been doing some thinking on the farm woman's place and wondering if she knows and has taken the place that rightfully belongs to her.
>
> Every good farm woman is interested as much in the business part of farm life as she is in the housework. . . .
>
> As soon as we can manage our household to give us the time, I think we should step out into this wider field, taking our place beside our husbands in the larger business of the farm. Co-operation, mutual help and understanding are the things that will make farm life what it should be.[18]

This theme of self-assertion and women's importance to the farm business permeates Wilder's columns over their entire run. She stressed that women should recognize that they had the power to do something about their lives, and their places on farms allowed them that opportunity. "It belittles us to think of our daily tasks as small things and, if we continue to do so, it will in time make us small," Wilder wrote in 1923. "It will narrow our horizon and make of our work just drudgery."[19] She argued that women must recognize the value of their own work and teach others to do so as well.

The subject of women's public roles was widely addressed in 1919. Farm women had played vital roles in producing food for the war effort, and after the war many young women apparently were heading to the cities. Wilder wrote with pride about the young women who worked in the factories, and she expressed happiness that women seemed to at last be gaining respect. "It makes our hearts thrill and our heads rise proudly to think that women were found capable and eager to do such important work in the crisis of wartime days. I think that never again will anyone have the courage to say that women could not run world affairs if necessary."[20]

18. Wilder, "As a Farm Woman Thinks," *Ruralist,* March 15, 1922, in ibid., 267.
19. Wilder, "As a Farm Woman Thinks," *Ruralist,* May 15, 1923, in ibid., 288–89.
20. Wilder, "Who'll Do the Women's Work?" *Ruralist,* April 5, 1919, in ibid., 180.

However, she cautioned that women should not leave their own "special" work behind. If women simply stopped doing what they had done for centuries—caring for home and children—no one else would do it. And that would present two problems: women would lose the ground they had gained, being forced back into the home, and future generations would be in deep trouble, "for the commonplace, home work of women is the very foundation upon which everything else rests. So if we wish to go more into world affairs, to have the time to work at public work, we must arrange our old duties in some way so that it will be possible. . . . Perhaps if we study conditions of labor and the forward movements of the world as related to the farm, we may find some way of applying the best of them to our own use."[21]

The point, for Wilder, was that women must take their places publicly, in voting booths and in political organizations. Some way had to be found to free women from the work that shackled them to the farms because they had other important work to do. "Farm women have been patient," Wilder wrote, "and worked very hard. It has seemed sometimes as though they and their work were overlooked in the march of progress. Yet improvement has found them out and a great many helps in their work have been put into use in the last few years."[22] With attention to their self-improvement, education, and socialization, women could organize and help each other with their work. "Modern" conveniences could pave the way, but the strong community spirit among these women would help them to improve their lives. Women's place in the home could not be supplanted, but women could also play a role in the world outside their farmhouse doors. Wilder said women needed to take their rightful place—beside their husbands, not behind them—and teach the world the value of their work.

This theme, of successful farms having successful partnerships between men and women, also was apparent in a 1920 article about homemaking on the farm written by "A Farmer's Wife" for *Ladies' Home Journal.* "Farmer and wife are partners literally from the ground up if they are the right sort of people, intimately associated in all their work both inside and outside the house in a way that few other husbands and wives have to be. . . . To be a success, their work must go hand in hand," the author asserted. In 1925, home economic training through government

21. Ibid., 180–81.

22. Wilder, "Shorter Hours for Farm Women," *Ruralist,* June 28, 1913, in ibid., 23.

programs was cited by at least one writer as significant to farm women's work: "This kind of knowledge has vastly increased the economic standing of rural women," Alice Ames Winter wrote in January.[23]

The Imagined Community

Farm journals such as *The Farmer's Wife* could bring farm women together through their pages in an era when geographic distance between farms might have made forming social clubs like those found in urban areas difficult. Through reader/writer participation in these journals, farm women built what Benedict Anderson in the 1980s called an "imagined community." For farm women who subscribed to *The Farmer's Wife,* the "Home Club" section provided an opportunity to converse with—and support—other women in a growing network through letters written not just to journal editors but to each other. In the geographic isolation associated with farming, this monthly "gathering" provided a vehicle for women to cope with the work and stress of farm life. Mrs. L. C. W. of Ohio wrote in May 1912: "Dear Sisters: This is indeed an interesting club with its monthly gatherings and Mrs. Farnsworth [the editor] is so courteous, too. We farmers' wives are always so busy that it is not possible to attend a mothers' club were we in touch with one and thus the 'Farmer's Wife' is doubly appreciated."[24]

Mrs. A. M. Ellis of North Dakota shared her recipe for fruit cake in 1911 before describing her North Dakota home:

> I also want to add that I enjoy The Farmer's Wife very much and especially the Home Club. I would like to tell other farmers' wives about this wonderful country that is settling up so fast. It is nearly three years since we came and it is far from being the desert waste it was always supposed to be. We have plenty of near neighbors, a nice new school house, where we hold Sunday school and a Christian Endeavor Society. The roads are being established and bridges built as fast as possible. We have a tri-weekly mail and a small store one and one-half miles away, so although we are 18 miles from the railroad, we are doing well and are contented until we can do better.[25]

23. A Farmer's Wife, "Making a Home on the Farm," *Ladies' Home Journal,* September 1920, 21; Winter, "Splendid Government Service if You Ask," *Ladies' Home Journal,* January 1925, 93.
24. "Our Home Club," *The Farmer's Wife,* May 1912, 376.
25. "Our Home Club," *The Farmer's Wife,* October 1911, 146.

Another, signing herself "A Reader," wrote in June 1913: "Dear Home Club: I am a farmer's wife and do enjoy reading your little paper very much. We live in the western part of this [unidentified] state where we can boast of rattle snakes and prairie dogs. This community is well settled. My nearest neighbor lives half a mile away. We live 15 miles from town. So you may imagine I do not go shopping very often."[26]

The system of friendly exchange built through the pages of such journals as *The Farmer's Wife* provided women an outlet for airing concerns and a space for asking questions of others who might have more experience in all manner of things—health, child rearing, farming, business practices, politics, or marital relations. The readers' column served as a kitchen table around which all the women could share a cup of coffee or tea and have a nice chat, as Mrs. Emma Beal suggested in 1911. "Dear Home Club: I like to drop in once in awhile and have a visit," she wrote in April. She outlined her daughter's tonsils problem and asked if osteopathy, rather than surgery, might correct the condition. "Can that be so? Is Osteopathy a reputable mode of treatment? Have any of the Farmer's Wife sisters had experience with it and can they tell me?" Other kinds of conversations are illustrated by the following excerpts from the same issue:

"Dear Home Club: Will one of the sisters give me a good recipe for mushroom catsup? There is nothing about it in my cook book," wrote Mrs. G. of Texas.

"Dear Home Club: The Farmer's Wife grows better with each number. My heart revels in our garden work and the page by Miss Dartt in the last number just brought me unfading joy. Tomatoes and celery are two things I have 'studied very deeply' and we have had splendid luck in their improvement each year. Now we are planning to try a hand at winter mushroom and rhubarb raising. If anyone has first-hand experience at their pencil point, we shall be glad to read it," wrote Jenny January.

"Dear Farmer's Wife: There is something so warmly helpful in Mrs. Goodwill's Mothers' Club in last [*sic*] number that someway [*sic*] I want to put my thanks on paper. When she brought the fathers into the meeting and expressed their sentiments on paper, she touched the heart of helpfulness in social clubs. We know from experience in our home what the revival of social meetings in our neighborhood has done in many other homes, but it was a one-sided effort until we got the men interested. Now it is a

26. "Our Home Club," *The Farmer's Wife*, June 1913, 42.

balanced, co-operative work in which we all take pride. We have been able to make our homes more interesting for our children, and in turn they have taken an increased interest in us and all their home surroundings. May Mrs. Goodwill's good work go on," "Prairie Mother" wrote.[27]

Time was a factor for women caught in the rush of work that accompanied the growing seasons. Some took the time to write long letters addressing multiple queries at once. For example, June Viola wrote, "What a dandy letter 'A Washington Subscriber' writes—but I say if a woman is capable of voting on the school and saloon questions, why isn't she able to study and vote on other matters? . . . Anna Rathbun, Ill, I'm sure I hope your osteopathy cure is permanent . . . Good for you 'Mountain Wind, Col.'—you roasted that Tennessee husband a plenty. I hope it did him good. . . . Well I must not close without giving helpful hints in return for some I've had: . . . I find an old pancake turner far better than a knife in cleaning the bottom of spiders and kettles."[28]

These conversations included opinions about family roles and requests for practical tips. "Cherry Blossom" wrote in 1912: "Dear Home Club: I am glad the Club women are getting down to the practical point of life in studying how to educate their children to earn a living. . . . Every girl ought to be taught how to keep house, and if possible be somewhat familiar if not proficient in some other line of work to her taste so that if ever she is thrown upon her own resources she will have something to fall back upon. Every boy should be taught some trade or profession, and it should play largely to his credit if he had some training in Domestic Science so as to help a wife regulate the household expense bills." "I used to be a farmer's wife but since my husband's death I live in town but am still a farm woman," wrote Mrs. LMG of Virginia in 1913. "I wish to do something for pin money. May I make one suggestion, dear Editor? It would be so nice if you could devote a small portion of 'the farmer's wife' to women making money at home."[29]

In 1912, the editors of *The Farmer's Wife* designated a "Home Club" editor, Annis Farnsworth, to collect and answer readers' letters. This seems to have stimulated more letters. Farnsworth arranged the letters and sometimes added her own notes. "Perhaps some of our readers can make some suggestions about decorating and celebrating for a tin

27. "Our Home Club," *The Farmer's Wife*, April 1911, 332.
28. "Our Home Club," *The Farmer's Wife*, October 1911, 146.
29. "Our Home Club," *The Farmer's Wife*, February 1912, 278; March 1913, 330.

wedding," she suggested at the end of one letter in 1913. Other suggestions were less innocuous. "Bachelor John," for example, said he hadn't much patience with the lot of women that he had met in California, "representative, as they put it of '900,000' club women," and said he would "like to know what other fathers and mothers and bachelors and maids think about such things." Farnsworth responded: "We like Bachelor John's frank way of expressing his opinions but will leave it for our readers to pass upon the opinions themselves."[30]

She also occasionally suggested topics that women could write about to the magazine. This note, in August 1912, illustrates: "Can we not hear from different farm mothers as to their plans for reading matter in their homes? It is soon coming winter when this subject should be one of heart to heart consideration." And she made statements that invited comments, too: "Since these farm children go out in such large numbers to make the world's workers, it is undeniable that the mother, and particularly the farm mother, is one of the most important factors in this great and growing United States."[31]

Particularly interesting were the discussions of citizenship and participation in civic affairs. In the regular "Home Club" column, women expressed cautious optimism about the suffrage movement, and some in favor of the vote wrote quite sharply—seemingly without much hope that things would change significantly. One reader in September 1913 complained of the isolation on the farms and of the repressive nature of her marriage. She never had a "cent of her own" and hadn't gone to see her family in nearly a year, despite living only twelve miles from them. "Encouraging, isn't it? I hope women of this and other countries get the ballot, and when they do, I hope husbands who make slaves of their wives, and refuse to share with them the pleasures within their reach, will be compelled to pay them wages," she declared, signing herself "Another Wife."[32]

Contrasting Constructions of Farm Women

Between 1930 and 1950, two contrasting views of life on the farm were seen in publications studied. The Great Depression, coupled with successive years of drought and crop failures, made 1930 conditions

30. "Bachelor John Speaks," *The Farmer's Wife,* August 1912, 90.
31. "Our Home Club," *The Farmer's Wife,* August 1912, 90.
32. "Our Home Club," *The Farmer's Wife,* September 1913, 124.

unbearable on many farms. The woman in Dorothea Lange's photograph is emblematic of those who were simply unable to succeed; such farm women were constructed as victims of hard work and poverty.

However, a contrasting view of farm women as successful stresses their self-reliance, hard work, and patience with unfavorable farming conditions. Rose Wilder Lane, born in 1886, a successful freelance journalist and fiction author by 1930, was angered by the U.S. government approach to dealing with the Great Depression. Virulently anti–New Deal, Lane wrote a series of editorials for *Woman's Day* magazine directed toward all women. It should be noted that Lane left Rocky Ridge Farm in 1903, at age seventeen, and has been characterized as "cosmopolitan."[33] However, after travels that took Lane to San Francisco, New York, Paris, France, and Albania, she returned to the farm in the late 1920s. She wrote much of her published political rhetoric while living at Rocky Ridge Farm during the 1930s. The farming culture in which she grew up and to which she later contributed shaped her views, which in her later years grew radically conservative. To Lane, capitalism, individualism, and self-reliance were the only ways to truly enjoy freedom—and she said so in her writing and apparently to anyone who would listen.

Lane's "Credo," published in the *Saturday Evening Post* in 1936, outlined her experiences with communism in Europe and argued for the exercise of freedom and American liberty. Followed by *The Discovery of Freedom: Man's Struggle against Authority* (1941), "Credo" articulated a sense of purpose for Lane, who abandoned fiction writing and focused nearly exclusively on political work. She wrote that "nothing whatever but the constitutional law, the political structure, of these United States protects any American from arbitrary seizure of his property and his person, from the Gestapo and the Storm Troops, from the concentration camp, the torture chamber, the revolver at the back of his neck in a cellar."[34]

This sense of purpose was evident as Lane began writing for *Woman's Day* when it was founded in 1937 as a giveaway flyer for the A&P grocery chain. Acquainted with magazine editor Eileen Tighe, Lane knew she could write, essentially, whatever she wanted.[35] "Don't Send Your

33. See William Holtz, *The Ghost in the Little House: A Life of Rose Wilder Lane.*

34. Rose Wilder Lane, "Credo," *Saturday Evening Post,* December 1936; available as "Give Me Liberty" at http://www.fff.org/freedom/0790d.asp (accessed 2008).

35. She says as much in a November 7, 1963, letter to Jasper Crane, reprinted in *The Lady and the Tycoon: The Best of Letters between Rose Wilder Lane and Jasper Crane,* ed. Roger Lea MacBride (Caldwell, Idaho: Caxton Printers, 1973).

Son to College," in August 1938, advocated allowing young people to work for their educations so they would succeed in life. Lane believed that young people without any exposure to life's challenges would lose ambition. She wrote about her adopted son:

> He had been segregated from hazards, as if in an army or a jail. Nothing had called upon his last reserves of energy. He could not study intensely through a summer and skip a grade, as I did more than once to save time and money; only so many hours in a classroom will get a unit. For ten years, he had been utterly unable to change his environment, whether he liked it or not. He had no experience in actual life, where he must depend upon his own efforts, where bare survival may exhaust his last ounce of determination and creative energy, where success demands fierce resolution, self-discipline, concentration, and where it is man's business to attack his environment and change it.[36]

Lane attributed her own success to her childhood struggles on the farm and her willingness to do whatever work was necessary to support herself. In the absence of government initiatives and city structures, such as transit and welfare systems, Lane had learned that success depended on hard work, luck, and pluck—and she viewed the "modern" culture of the late 1930s as steadily depriving people of the opportunity to learn such lessons. For example, "Don't Tell Me How to Live My Life," in September 1939, criticized a culture that she saw as increasingly relying on advice from "experts" for basic living skills.

> Today you can't pick up a new magazine or go into a bookshop without being told in print how to be popular, how to make friend, how to live alone or get a husband, how to hang onto him when you've got him, how to get along with his mother, how to bring up the children (and precisely what kind of children you must make them be), how to make home happy, how to make a guest feel welcome in your house, or how to be a welcome guest, how to treat an adopted child, how to keep your friends. Never before was every woman so thoroughly told how to live.[37]

"We Women Are Not Good Citizens," in March 1939, chided women for not being more politically involved. "Own Your Own Home," published in January 1939, forcefully posited that young couples should work

36. Lane, "Don't Send Your Son to College," *Woman's Day,* August 1938, 4–5, 44.
37. Lane, "Don't Tell Me How to Live My Life," *Woman's Day,* September 1939, 6–7.

harder and live with some sacrifices in order to own a piece of land and make a decent living. As the country entered World War II, Lane took on conscription and compulsory military training, saying that the best candidates for military service were volunteers, not conscripts.[38]

Perhaps it was Lane's upbringing on the hardscrabble farm in the Ozarks that instilled in her a conviction that freedom—defined as freedom from government interference in life—can only be enjoyed when people suffer for it. Individualism, for her, was a cornerstone of American liberty. Lane's rhetoric is that of a woman who fled the farm but was nonetheless shaped by the experience of farm life.

Letters to *Farmer's Wife* during this period reflect the same sort of rhetoric, but in less extreme terms. The letters express the belief that farming success relied on individualism and freedom from government interference and that farm life, despite difficulties with overwork and lack of educational opportunities, still offered the best chance for success and happiness. At least some letters seemed to say that farm women had the the same opportunity as men to fail or succeed on their own, to raise large and loving families, and, with the help of God, live a useful life, if not an easy one. Many agreed, for example, that while farm women's work at home was invaluable, both farm women and men had to work away from the farm as well as on the farm. Many farm women worked two jobs—one on the farm, maintaining a household and a business, and one in town, adding to household income. In August 1930, Mrs. I. R. of New York wrote in response to "Harriet Farmer": "I think you are right about homemaking being the most important work for the wife if the husband is unable to secure the income. But so pitifully many things can combine to hinder that. In such a case, it isn't so bad for the wife to go back to teaching as to be obliged to take in washings as countless women have done."[39]

One letters column, called "On the Party Line," offered off-the-cuff responses to previous letters, in a fashion similar to contemporary Internet forums. The women who wrote to the magazines, despite the enormous amount of work they faced in their everyday lives, had to make

38. "We Women Are Not Good Citizens," *Woman's Day,* March 1939; "Own Your Own Home," *Woman's Day,* January 1939, 7, 44ff.; "We Who Have Sons," *Woman's Day,* December 1939, 4–5, 41ff.; "Force Won't Keep the Peace," *Woman's Day,* February 1945, 29, 86ff.

39. "To the Last Ounce of Their Strength," *The Farmer's Wife,* August 1930, 16.

time to write for, and read, the columns. Their opinions and interests have the strength of conviction behind them. The columns convey that farm women viewed themselves as partners with their husbands in the farming business and were vital to farming's success and innovative in approaching business.

Farm Women in the Postwar Era

Of the six magazines studied for this research, *Good Housekeeping* had no letters columns between 1940 and 1960, *Ladies' Home Journal* had a limited number of letters from readers, and the *Saturday Evening Post* had none in the issues studied. By contrast, the farming magazines all maintained letters columns; the *Farm Journal,* in particular, had three such columns throughout this period, including two in *The Farmer's Wife* half of the magazine. This suggests that the geographic isolation of the farm homes led readers to use these media for connecting with others in similar situations. In the process they built an imagined community.

Letters were found in the 1940, 1945, 1950, 1955, and 1960 issues of the *Farm Journal* and *The Farmer's Wife* examined for this research. In additional previous research, letters from selected months of 1956, 1957, 1958, 1959, 1961, and 1962 also were studied.[40] Although farm women contributed to the features and editorial columns, as outlined in the previous chapter, among all the sources examined their letters may best reveal the farming culture. Most of the magazine content read neglected farm women's interests and directed them toward a homemaker role. But these letters columns gave farm women in the 1950s an outlet for expressing their interests, ambitions, and values. Letters to *The Farmer's Wife,* read for years between 1950 and 1962, discuss ideas and topics of interest to a specific culture of women who shared a collective identity as farmer's wives and women farmers.

Individualism, farming as a business important to the global arena, and farming as a way of life were discussed in letters to the *Farm Journal* and to *The Farmer's Wife.* Women's work was also discussed as being vital to the farming business and to farm life, and by extension women were

40. This research was presented as "'We Are Legion': Community-Building and *The Farmer's Wife,* 1955–1962" at the American Journalism Historians Association annual conference in 2005.

discussed as themselves needing care. These discussions reflected the discontent of some farm women with the domesticity associated with their roles on the farms.

The idea of women's work as vital to farm life, seen clearly in the *Farm Journal,* was very much emphasized in *The Farmer's Wife.* For example, the occupations listed by Mrs. Arnold Bender, the South Dakota farmer's wife quoted in Chapter 2, included veterinarian, budgeteer, banker, poultry culler, painter, plumber, lawnmower, hunter, mechanic, and photographer—roles that indicate her place on the farm was not simply domestic.

Farm women were also discussed as successful entrepreneurs in their own rights on the farms. For example, Veva Rawlings wrote in May 1956 about how she started and maintained a business selling iris bulbs: "Well, I have done all the work required of a farm wife, and cared for my iris garden and mail-order business in iris bulbs. It's kept me busy, but in 12 years I made as much profit from my one-fourth acre as we paid for our 107-acre farm."[41] Other farm women's tasks discussed included poultry raising, gardening, sewing, and boarding summer "guests." Some women wrote about jobs away from the farm that they had taken to help make ends meet, or about such jobs as bookkeeping that they performed on the farm in addition to their domestic tasks.

But tensions about filling dual roles were seen in several letters. For example, Y. Wilson of New York wrote the following in January 1961 after a church sermon that critiqued her for being a working mother:

> I just came home from church, and I'm mad. Today the sermon was on Juvenile Delinquency, and the minister gave working mothers as a cause of this tragedy. Well, I'm a working mother and I'd like to speak up for thousands of decent, hard-working moms and their well-behaved children. Those of us who work show our love by doing something for our families. Many times at work when things go wrong I'd like to chuck my job. Then I remember how much my family depends on me. Many [livestock] feed bills have been paid with my salary check. I think it is unfair for educators, clergyman and other leaders to take this unfortunate attitude. It's time we working mothers got credit for what we are trying to do.[42]

41. "Loveliness for Sale," *The Farmer's Wife,* May 1956, 167.
42. "Working Mom Speaks Her Mind," *The Farmer's Wife,* January 1961, 67.

And Doris Knox of North Dakota wrote in July of 1961: "Oh, that housekeeping had the same appeal as an office job, so that it would be possible to hire occasional household help. Maybe a short course in home-making with a diploma would dignify the position of 'day workers.'"[43]

Juanita Yates in May 1956 listed bookkeeper and banker among her trades:

> When you have six children—and I do—you're neck-deep in two dozen careers! . . . I am a bookkeeper and banker for a busy husband; nutritionist and cook, seamstress and photographer. I am maker of dolls, repairer of toys, counselor for broken hearts. I am teacher, baseball umpire in season, vegetable gardener and grower of roses. I am hair-dresser, chicken and rabbit raiser, sometime-football coach, story-teller and reader of poems.

But Yates also voiced her discouragement with the work she had to do and the use to which she was putting her college education: "(My college courses in speech serve a purpose which I little anticipated when I took them.) I am often tired, sometimes discouraged, seldom free for contemplation, often distracted, never up-to-date with the reading I want to do."[44]

The letter writers' descriptions of work on the farms show that women's work was productive and that women had to balance their roles as working parents with meeting personal needs. Women took pride in their work on the farms, and they knew they were making important contributions to both household and business—each of which fed the other.

Women were discussed also simply as people, rather than just as wives and mothers. This was seen in many letters offering encouragement and support for tired young mothers and tips for helping all women find time for themselves. Despite freezers full of farm-raised beef and cellars full of produce, some praised convenience foods as opportunities to "buy time" away from cooking. Some suggested education and other forms of self-improvement as ways for women to focus on themselves as women—not as wives. A delicate balance of domestic obligations against personal needs was often clear in letters. For example, Georgia farmwife Dorothy Lane wrote in September 1960, "Why shouldn't I study and improve myself as long as this ambition doesn't interfere

43. "Quotes," *The Farmer's Wife*, July 1961, 70.
44. "My Careers," *The Farmer's Wife*, May 1956, 166.

with my home life?" Another example is a March 1959 article based on letters responding to M. M. of Washington, who had expressed her discouragement with her role as a young mother on a farm. Titled "Be a Person, Not a Mommy," the article offered such suggestions as letting a husband babysit the children for an afternoon. The mother might simply enjoy the respite or take a warm bubble bath. Another idea was to trade work with other young women with the same needs in the neighborhood. Another was that she should force her husband to listen to her concerns—by listening to his. "Getting the man to talk, and listen, could lead to a wife-saving kitchen appliance or an allowance for a sitter," one woman wrote. M. M. was told that if she did not take care of herself, she couldn't possibly take care of anybody else.[45]

Letter writers also discussed how women managed personal problems, which ranged from "perpetual" pregnancies and childbirth to drunken spouses. One woman wrote in October 1958:

> Prices low, crops bad, hay spoiled, cow swallowed hardware. I have learned to live with such news and stretch my work-away-from-home paycheck with little whimpering. But at times we have a situation that I'm unable to cope with. My husband goes on drinking sprees. Each time there are tears, heartaches, quarrels, expense and later regrets and apologies from an otherwise very fine husband. All suggestions for a lasting cure fall on deaf ears. I am as defeated as if he had an incurable disease. Can anyone who has had the same experience tell me what to do?[46]

Writing to *The Farmer's Wife* could be cathartic as women unburdened themselves of their deepest problems, sometimes withholding names, and asked other readers for help. The anonymity of some letters may have been a safety measure used by women fearful of seeking advice in a public venue. Problems seem to have been familiar to all letter writers, and the women offered each other support through their own experiences. Strategies were suggested for how an individual woman could effect change within her own household, often through the manipulation of her husband. A farm woman's domesticity and her role as a domestic were as unquestioned as was her role as a businesswoman.

The columns of letters read show how *The Farmer's Wife* aided farm

45. "Why Not More Education?" *The Farmer's Wife,* September 1960; Maude Longwell, "Be a Person, Not a Mommy," *The Farmer's Wife,* March 1959, 90.

46. "Husband on a Binge," *Farm Journal* 82:10 (October 1958): 75.

women in building networks of community. One letter, mentioned earlier, generated fifteen hundred responses, which were published in a special edition of *The Farmer's Wife* that addressed the concerns of the initial letter writer. First published in 1958, the letter reads in part:

> Dear Editor: Last night I had company—a woman whom I like very much. But I couldn't be at ease. My house was a mess. That's so often how it is; I almost dread the sound of car wheels on our driveway. I work hard, day after day, go out very little. But I have so little to show for my work that in spite of everything I feel like I failed. . . . Many young women are in the same spot. So much that must be done, so little time to do it. We find that we have less to manage with when the children are small and extra help is needed than when we are older. Out of the wealth of experience so many other farm women have had, can your readers give me some pointers on how to manage with some degree of efficiency? I've wrestled with this problem alone year in and year out—without success so far. Now, I'm asking for help. —M.M., Washington[47]

In noting the burden of work she carried as a young farmer's wife, M. M. did not question that the burden was hers. Instead, she asked for help from the extended network of farm women who had been where she was, as overwhelmed young mothers. Women responded in large numbers, filling the entire March 1959 issue of *The Farmer's Wife.*

Laura Lane, an editor for the journal, compiled the responses into an article that encapsulated the tensions associated with women's roles on farms. Among suggestions offered in the letters were making husbands share housework as much as the women shared farmwork, women asserting themselves and demanding the help and respect they needed, and subtly manipulating spouses to get the tools women needed to help in their work. All letters seem to have acknowledged that M. M.'s situation was not unique and needed to be addressed. The article compiled from the letters ended with a positive note from a farm woman who told M. M. she was not alone—that she was all farm women: "Remember, too, you aren't wrestling with your problem alone. Writing this, I feel such a kinship with you. I don't know whether you have dark hair or light, whether you have a tendency to overeat (I do), what you like to read. But I love you, because you are me, and we are legion."[48]

47. "Work Never Done!" *The Farmer's Wife,* January 1958, 75–76.
48. Laura Lane, "How Does a Young Wife Manage?" *Farmer's Wife,* March 1959, 111.

Although these women were separated by geography and isolated on their farmsteads, they felt connected via the magazine in a supportive network not unlike the kinship networks that scholars, such as John Mack Farragher, have called vital to farm life. The letters and the strength and force of the conversations via the columns in the *Farm Journal* and *The Farmer's Wife* reveal a community of people tied together by common interests and by a common publication.

The letters also reveal that the editors' attempts to make farming as a profession attractive to women could not succeed. The amounts of work and the lack of cash for leisure, labor-saving devices, and educational opportunities made women look for more than farm life could offer. Although many women chose to stay on farms to maintain their business partnerships with their husbands, those who did not stay had viable and legitimate reasons for wanting to leave. In an urban environment where work was confined to basic domestic tasks, leisure could be found just steps away, and a woman could keep herself clean and pretty. In contrast, farm women, though respected, were overworked, underpaid, and unable to participate in urban leisure activities to the degree they might have liked.

Women's letters to the *Farm Journal* column addressed a variety of subjects. Women contributed significantly to this column between 1950 and 1962, and they discussed different subjects than did the men who wrote to the *Farm Journal*. However, the way in which they discussed issues was similar. Men's letters focused on farm business, politics, progress, techniques, and economics. Key issues during the time included uses for farm surpluses, government aid to farmers (was it communist?), land reclamation (was that communist?), and which political parties did more for the farmer. Women occasionally contributed to these discussions, but they usually discussed farm family life, education, and reproduction. The same ideology of individualism, Americanism, and the importance of farming was seen in letters from both men and women.

Men and women wrote with suspicion about initiatives that appeared to call for collective action. For example, three women wrote in December 1960 to express their opinions under the title "Should Farmers Unionize?" Mrs. Riley Hill, of Pleasant Hill, Missouri, personalized the issue: "Why does the buyer tell the farmer how much he'll pay? I've always been told the price if I wanted to buy. The National Farm Organization could really help the farm *if he'd let it*." Barbara Gowin of Hettick, Illinois, said collective action should not take away farmers' individuality. "Farmers unionize? Perhaps they should, but not if, in so doing, they no longer think as individuals. We country folk have long been proud that we think for ourselves; any organization which robs us of such initiative cannot be for our own good."[49]

Part of the objection to collective action in these years rested on cold war arguments against "communist" or "socialist" politics. "It will take more than public relations and singing commercials [to encourage farm families to organize]," L. E. McDonald wrote in April 1960. "Farmers are the only evidence left of individual initiative."[50]

Tension was evident in discussions of whether farm aid would be considered communist, and whether that was good or bad. For farmers to keep their status as successful businesspeople, some argued, farm aid was necessary, and that was not communistic. "Private enterprise just doesn't work fairly for the farmer now," wrote H. E. Dorsey in December 1957. "He can't compete with union labor and corporation wealth":

> Your accusation that plans for government farm aid are communist is far-fetched. Such plans are no more *socialistic* than many measures that aid labor and industry today. The family farm can't be maintained without government aid and supervision. And without the family farm, we will revert to medieval-like days, with gigantic corporation farms and all farmers in the roles of serfs.[51]

"What's Wrong with Agriculture?" headlined an August 1957 letter from Mrs. William L. Hill, who said men like her husband with rural upbringing and experience couldn't get into farming without some kind of aid. "How can he even dream of a farm, let alone maintain a decent standard of living for his family on his DHIA [Dairy Herd Information Association] sales of $200 a month?" she asked.[52]

Women writers also discussed the dangers associated with farming, especially for children. Children, they wrote, must be protected from the many perils on the farm: lack of adequate supervision because of adults' heavy workloads, the tendency to allow children to operate tractors and other machines, and the risks associated with farming equipment. Mrs.

49. "Should Farmers Unionize?" *Farm Journal* 84:12 (December 1960): 18 (emphasis in original).

50. "Win Friends?" *Farm Journal* 84:4 (April 1960): 27.

51. "Back to the Middle Ages?" *Farm Journal* 81:12 (December 1957): 26.

52. "What's Wrong with Agriculture?" *Farm Journal* 81:8 (August 1957): 18.

Charley Stoneking wrote urgently in July 1961 regarding the need to keep children away from dangerous farm equipment: "But until they are old enough to think for themselves, we have to think for them. Find something for your children to do in the yard where you can watch them. It's too late for my precious boy. But it's not too late for yours."[53]

Issues raised by men and women about communism and farm aid characterize an era when many Americans feared the threat of a nuclear war with the Soviet Union. Farmers debated their roles in that larger global arena and discussed farmwork, especially food production, as important to the American cause. The following excerpt from one heated exchange about farm aid illustrates the issue: "One farmer retires his land for pay, while down the road another accepts ACP [Agricultural Conservation Program] money to build his farm up. These Government programs are smothering each other," Mrs. James Weidman wrote in May 1962. Jim Johnson responded: "You voice the consensus of farmers around here in wanting to eliminate Federal intervention." And Carl Burmeister interjected: "You ought to pay me to read these poison pen attacks on our government." Another writer said, "I keep seeing the words 'cooperator' and 'non-cooperator.' What a nasty term for someone who only wants to mind his own business. Why not unemotional words—participator and non-participator, for example?"[54]

The fear of a nuclear war might also have provoked the disgust with which some farm men and women wrote about the atomic age as a significant problem to be overcome. "Acts of God may not be prevented, but to accept *man-made* disaster of atomic warfare glibly and supinely is deplorable," A. A. Fraser wrote in May 1960. In the same column, Wendell Clampit asked, "How can we get the people to see the real civil defense—which is to abolish nuclear weapons?" Mrs. Alfred Boeckmann pleaded for better understanding of the issues and for collective action: "Only a few of us can work and talk to shape world policies. But all can be vitally concerned—to live peacefully, even in small groups, read and know, tolerate and understand those that irk us."[55]

Underlying many letters was the view of farming as a business and as a way of life. Men who wrote to *Farm Journal* supported and respected women's contributions to the column, to the farm, and to the home. In

53. "Please—Heed the Warning!" *Farm Journal* 85:7 (July 1961): 18.
54. "More on Our Poll," *Farm Journal* 86:5 (May 1962): 14.
55. "Survival," *Farm Journal* 84:5 (May 1960): 31.

one letter a woman complained about her husband not appreciating the work she put into cooking, and the male editor of the letters column suggested that she try starving him. Another man, after his visit to a farm, expressed admiration for the work farm women did. Ardell Countryman (probably a pseudonym) wrote, "Mrs. Smith was operating a tractor and disk at top speed . . . and his hired man's wife was feeding the 300 to 400 cattle! Mr. Smith actually had *three* hired men!"[56]

Some letters sparked debate about women's working roles off the farm. In February 1962, Ruth Van Lien angrily took issue with an article in *The Farmer's Wife* that suggested farm women go away from the farms to find work to supplement family incomes. In a letter to *Farm Journal*, she wrote: "I resent being told to find a new way to make money to pay farm bills [The Farmer's Wife, Nov. 1961]. Our farm is a business and is supposed to pay its own bills as well as make a profit. Why should we break our health on two jobs? We should get a fair price for products—and [not] have to make money some other place to pay bills."[57]

Study of the letters reviewed suggests that letters columns served an important function. Editors regularly asked readers to respond to letters and features, and they often grouped responses in subsequent columns. *Farm Journal* appears to have been important to community building, and the population the journal served seems to have consisted of literate, educated, thoughtful people with common purposes and shared interests in farming. These letters reveal that farm women constructed themselves as businesswomen, central to the farm home and community and respected for the work they did. However, farm women also discussed themselves as being overworked and in need of self-care. In the next chapter, the contributions of women who lived through this period—their oral history and correspondence—bear out the constructions of farm women found in these texts.

56. "Should She Starve Him?" *Farm Journal* 81:6 (June 1957): 18; "Don't Forget the Ladies!" *Farm Journal* 86:2 (February 1962): 18.

57. No subhead, *Farm Journal* 86:2 (February 1962).

6

Passing It On

Talking to women today about their experiences on the farm between 1910 and 1960 reveals how strong those memories truly are. Commonalities surrounding the main tasks on the farm, including the production of food for consumption or sale, and the main roles for women, including partnership in the business production, reveal the extent to which the constructions found in farm magazines are borne out through women's lived experiences.

But the women themselves raise important points that problematize the optimism demonstrated in the magazines. While many who lived on strong, sustainable farms spoke positively about their experiences, others did not. The main differences between the two camps seem to have been the degree of farming business knowledge, the general geographic region, and ownership versus tenancy on farmland. Women whose experiences closely followed those expressed in the magazines—that is, they were business partners on a large farm with a sustainable, diversified income—had the most positive experiences. Others who didn't own their own land, or who attempted to start farms during this period without substantial start-up funds, had more negative experiences. In other words, the key to positive experiences for farm women seems to have been the success of the farm business.

An example comes from Florence Bley of Ohio:

> We moved to a 20-acre farm with a 6-year-old girl and a 4-year-old boy in 1945. The bells were ringing one of the first days we started to clean up the house and we found out later that it was the end of the war. We moved from the city to the farm, so we could have goats for milk. We'd heard that goat milk would be good for my husband's ulcers.
>
> We moved in August 1945 and in June 1946 my husband's parents were killed in an auto accident and I went into shock and almost lost a little boy I was pregnant with.
>
> Bought 100 day-old chicks to raise for fryers. When they were about half raised we lost many to sickness. We had domestic rabbits we raised, killed and cleaned for meat.

> Another idea to have meat for ourselves was to raise two calves. Since we knew little about raising them we lost one because we didn't know you had to give them grain.
>
> When our 19-month-old son got Rocky Mountain Spotted Fever he was in the hospital for 11 days. That was in August and in December of the same year our 7-year-old daughter had a freak accident and was hospitalized for 10 days.
>
> After four years we were able to sell and start a small hardware store. (That's another story.)
>
> My daughter said that was four years of hell.[1]

Bley's story demonstrates that farm living, especially for those who were new to it or unfamiliar with it, could be an overwhelmingly negative experience, and such negative constructions are nowhere to be found in the farming magazines studied here. Bley's story also illustrates the importance of the interviews and correspondence conducted; a question raised by the research into the media constructions of farm women during this period was whether such constructions accurately reflected the lives of those women who experienced farm life firsthand. In order to find out, it was important to ask women what their experiences were, and to discuss the constructions found in the magazines with women who lived through that era on the farm. This task appears daunting; as women's historian Joan M. Jensen has noted, women who fled the farms appear reticent to discuss their experiences. Her acquaintance with women in northern Wisconsin demonstrated an unwillingness to reflect on farm life, in part, Jensen suggests, because of the hardships endured by those women.[2]

With this in mind, I started my task by engaging with my social networks, spreading word about who I sought and why. Women who were interested in contributing their experiences contacted me, and, when possible, I sought personal interviews in the women's homes or area coffee shops. Retirement communities invited me to talk about my work, and audience members who could—and wanted to—contribute to this research set up individual interviews with me. Additionally, *Country Woman* magazine, published by Reiman Publications in Greenfield, Wisconsin, agreed to include my request for women's stories and histories in its January/February 2007 issue. Within a day of its publication, emails

1. Bley, letter to author, July 24, 2007.
2. Jensen, "'I'd Rather Be Dancing': Wisconsin Women Moving On."

began pouring in; within a week, these emails were supplemented by postal letters that arrived by the dozens and included personal diaries, previously self-published memoirs, photographs, and press clippings from the period. Some simply wrote about their experiences, happy to pass them on, while others asked what, exactly, I sought. All of the women who responded to the request were contacted personally with a friendly questionnaire that asked five primary questions: What was your role on the farm? What was your life like? What kinds of publications and media were important in your everyday life? How did you/do you view city living? How do you define "city"? The women also were asked to talk about their views regarding advantages and disadvantages of farm living and to share a story about their farm experiences.

Two things became clear: these women were not reticent, and *Country Woman* provided a community-building function for its audience, just as had the farm magazines I'd studied. More than two hundred women or relatives of farm women contacted me from geographic locations across the United States and into Canada. More than half responded to the questionnaire, and several passed the questionnaire and request for stories on to others. Some who got in touch conducted interviews with their parents or grandparents, transcribed them, and sent them on. The response itself is part of the story to be told in this chapter. The request clearly touched a nerve from many who thought their history had been hidden for too long.

Mass Media on the Farm

One of the main questions asked of all participants was what role mass media played in their lives on the farms. Media served practical needs; newspapers, for example, served not just as vehicles for getting the news but also as raw material for cleaning supplies, kindling, dress-making, and other projects. When asked what subscriptions were kept, *Farm Journal* and *Progressive Farmer* were the top magazines taken by farm families, followed by local or regional farming publications, the county's extension bulletins or newsletters, and the local daily or weekly newspaper. In more affluent households, women also subscribed to *Ladies' Home Journal*, *Better Homes and Gardens*, or *Woman's Day*.

Less affluent families still took the local newspaper and county extension office bulletins but more often than not couldn't afford the subscription rates for the national magazines. Some looked to the free catalogs that came into their homes as sources of reading material and inspiration. The John Deere catalog, the Sears, Roebuck catalog, and the Montgomery Ward catalog headed the list of free publications read by many women. Another regional publication, *Capper's Weekly*, was also a popular choice. And many women noted the year in which radio had come to their farms, sometime in the 1920s, and the years when electricity, telephones, and televisions had made it into their farm homes. The arrival of these new technological tools of the twentieth century made a deep impression on those who witnessed it. In an interview in 2006, for example, Phyllis Spade still recalled the special procedures her farm family had had to employ to maintain their radio. "You did not just let the radio run because you would run the battery down," the Kansas native said. "When the battery ran down, you would take it to town, and they charged it, and during that time, you had no radio. So for a couple of days you had no radio contact."[3]

Some noted that mass media introduced alternate perspectives into farming culture that might have contributed to dissatisfaction with farm life. Helen Helder recalled having "adequate" clothing and food, but she blamed mass media for introducing farmers to consumer products that made them feel "poor" because they couldn't afford them. "There was no way of knowing if we were poor because everyone was in the same boat" before mass media told them differently, Helder noted. She added:

> Slowly our farm magazines introduced new methods of the future, but today we see daily how the whole world lives via the newscasts from the entire world. Television is great, but it has also caused those less fortunate to want what others have, thus feeling deprived, and dissatisfied. The ever-present quest for more possessions makes for poor folk in the midst of plenty.[4]

What's clear is that a reasonable correlation exists between the magazines read by the women surveyed here and the magazines studied here, and that these materials may be said to reflect the changing culture in which these women were raised. This does give weight to constructions identified in the previous chapters. Interviews and correspondence with women also reinforced other commonsense constructions for this community.

3. Spade, interview, September 11, 2006.
4. Helder, *In One Lifetime*, 16.

These snapshots of farm life find common ground; in the majority of responses, the stories were similar. But a more common initial response, especially from older farm women, centered on the same reluctance that Jensen noted in her study. Some contributors had difficulty getting their cherished elders to participate in the study. A common attitude was one of humility and bewilderment. My own Aunt Bonnie attempted several times to get her mother, Leone Alden, to open up about her life on the farm. "She doesn't seem to think anybody would care about her story," Bonnie wrote me. (I should note that, like scholar Joan Jensen's family, Bonnie's family—and mine—built farms in northern Wisconsin.) But Bonnie wasn't alone. Randall Weller expressed the same bewilderment on behalf of his mother in Missouri, but he pressed the issue, convinced that her history was worth telling. This humility seemed almost a function of the divide identified in the media of the period—by 1960, mainstream media no longer responded to farm women's needs or addressed them as a group. The women who sought participation in this study seemed to be accustomed to being overlooked.

While most of the women who chose to contribute to this research seemed to remember their lives on the farm with genuine affection, underscoring the centrality and importance of the farm woman to the business of farming, others seemed compelled to counter that affection with stories of overwork and escape. The women interviewed fell into two camps: those who loved farm life and those who loathed it. Interestingly, there appeared to be a relationship between the degree of education achieved by women and their increased loathing of farm life. Additionally, women who were raised on farms during the struggles of the economic depression of the 1930s seemed more likely to have left the farm upon maturity, citing the hard work and a need for another kind of career. Maternal health was a real struggle, and while women may have been respected by a certain class of reader and farmer, as reflected in the pages of the farming magazines, for others life on farms meant drudgery and potential loss of vitality, if not life. The difference seemed to be in the measure of farming successes, with those who were struggling to achieve affluence, rather than mere survival, responding more positively. The stories told by farm women both reinforced and contradicted the constructions of farm women found in the farming magazines.[5]

5. According to a February 1960 report from the U.S. Census bureau, literacy rates among the rural population in the United States were only slightly lower than those

An Impulse to Preserve

The impulse to preserve the way of life outlined in the stories and correspondence shared here reflects the idea that mainstream American culture has abandoned the farm.[6] There is a sense that these family stories, and these individual histories, need preservation so that future generations can learn from the experiences reflected in them. An entire underground movement in preservation and oral history appears to have taken up the cause articulated by Laura Ingalls Wilder when she first wrote "Pioneer Girl," the manuscript that became a sort of working outline for the Little House series of children's books. The history, as Wilder said at one point, was entirely too good to be lost.

Still, the range of the memoirs shared by the farm women who offered their stories in response to my questions in itself is interesting. In some cases, families sent cartons of old diaries, ledgers, and family photos; in others, carefully typed and assembled books and booklets—titled, copied, and bound for distribution—were sent with the idea that I might be able to use them. All it required to get such materials, it seems, was that someone should finally ask.

Beverly Aiken shared her mother-in-law's story through a eulogy she'd offered at the latter's funeral. Dola Glenn Aiken passed away just before the request to readers of *Country Woman* magazine for their stories was published. Beverly Aiken noted in her email that she thought I might be interested in Dola's story, written by her in 1984, because she was born in 1910 on a farm, lived on one for most of her life, and wrote down the stories of her parents and grandparents. "Family was her #1 priority," Aiken said. "She gave her never-ending support on whatever

---

among the urban population, and women farmers were more literate than men farmers. The overall rate of illiteracy in the United States in 1960 was reported as 2.2 percent; for farmers, the overall rate was 4.3 percent. Of all farmers, 5.6 percent of men and 2.9 percent of women were reported as illiterate. Overall, women had higher rates of literacy than did men, which suggests that men, being expected to work at younger ages, simply did not have the educational opportunities that women had. It's also possible that women valued education more than men did. This opens a line for further study. (Current Population Reports: Population Characteristics, Series P-20 no. 99, Washington D.C.: U.S. Department of Commerce Bureau of the Census, February 4, 1960).

6. Curiously, at the time of this writing, a new reality television show was airing on the CW Network. In *Farmer Takes a Wife,* a Missouri farmer puts several young women "through their paces" to determine whether any has what it takes to be a farmer's wife.

we chose to do. We could count on her being there, and be proud of us, no matter what."[7] Dola Aiken's personal story provided her descendants with significant material to document their family history.

In 2007, Melvin Buhrkuhl shared with me the private memoirs his mother had published for family members in 1996. He included a photocopy of his mother's handwritten memoirs, compiled from 1979 to 1983. "My mother loved to write and was the best speller I know," he confided. "I did not receive that gift and was a D student in English & spelling, but with a computer and spell check I get by. My mother left two footlockers full of family history." Gerry Evans, a third-generation rancher in South Dakota, sent fifty pages of memoir. "You never know where my musings might take me!" she added in a handwritten note on one page. Helen Helder not only wrote a book but she also had it published privately, donating copies to libraries in her Iowa City community. Her daughter, Irene Lary, shared her only remaining copy of that work, which was published in 1992. Helen passed away in 2003. "Mother would be so pleased to know someone is working on this!!!!!" Lary shared.[8]

About a third of the participants in this research already had prepared family memoirs, or had their parents' memoirs, to share with me as I looked into their history. Others, prompted by my questioning, found that they remembered a great deal more than they'd thought. Billie Hicks Parker, a Louisiana native, wrote that remembering her childhood had been "such fun" that she believed she'd write more down for her own "children and grand-angels."[9] Many who contributed believed that their history was in imminent danger of being lost because of the emphasis placed in mainstream culture on urban society, and were all too willing to share their perceptions of that history.

Women's Roles on the Farm

A common theme among all of the women was the hard work expected and required of farm women. Farm women and girls were responsible for work that included household tasks, cooking, and yard

7. Beverly Aiken, email to author, February 8, 2007.

8. Buhrkuhl, letter to author, January 6, 2007; Evans, letter to author, January 29, 2007; Lary, letter to author, January 29, 2007.

9. Parker, letter to author, February 15, 2007.

work but also business tasks. Chief among these was tending chickens and gardens to produce food for consumption and sale. Additionally, women needed to be well versed in all areas of the farming business and able to fill in at any task when needed.

June Dill,[10] who lived on a Kansas farm from her birth in 1941 until she turned eighteen and left for nursing school in 1959, said that in her household everyone had chores—specific farming tasks that needed to be done daily. "That is how they survived," Dill said. "It was anything from gathering eggs and feeding the chickens to having to milk cows in the summer in the evenings, getting the cows in." While women did the housework as a matter of course, they were also expected to milk cows, drive the tractor, and do multiple errands, especially at harvest time. "If the machine broke down, you had to be able to go to town to get the right parts and stuff like that," Dill recalled.[11]

Pat Betzen recalled her nearly forty years on the farm, from the time she was a new bride in 1951, with nostalgia and wit, and regarded her mother-in-law, with whom she and her husband lived, with respect bordering on awe. "His mother was the most wonderful woman I ever met," Betzen said. "She was a workhorse." Betzen continued:

> She was raising all the kids . . . she just lived in a one-room shack-like thing [early on]. She would get up and fry bacon and sausage and fix something real good for breakfast and then go to the barn and milk cows and then come in and feed the family and get the kids off to school and fix their lunches and get the men off to the field. Then she would have to go off to the barn, separate the milk, and start cooking. She went to the garden and picked her vegetables. At noon, they would usually just have sandwiches; their big meal was in the evening. In the morning, they would put the milk in 10-gallon milk cans and then take it to Woodward [Oklahoma] where people would buy the milk. Outside of dairying, they raised wheat.

Later in the conversation, Betzen listed what made her mother-in-law so "wonderful": "She didn't care about material things, she was a hard worker, and she saved money."[12] Notice the value placed on work, but

10. The women who are identified by name gave explicit written permission for their names to be used in the final work.

11. Dill, interview, September 2006.

12. Betzen, interview, September 2006.

also on a lack of concern for material objects. This attitude clashes with the blooming consumer culture of the time but highlights the central norms of those raised on a farm—norms that devalued the material and valued the effort that went into living.

Vivian Alexander remembered her mother's work raising a thousand chickens every year and her sideline business in the dairy, selling cream. "It wasn't the chief money-making of the farm, but the cream and the eggs were used for various things around the house and the other things that mother particularly wanted to buy," Alexander said. Although the soil on their Kansas farm wasn't conducive to raising garden produce, Alexander's mother tried out a garden spot every year, and vegetables were canned for winter eating. Peaches, strawberries, and cherries were bought in season for the same purpose. "One year my mother had surgery and she wasn't able to help me do much of the work," Alexander recalled. "So, I canned two crates of cherries, a crate of strawberries, and I think it was two bushels of peaches. I canned with very little supervision; I had to do it all myself. I was probably ten or eleven years of age at the time." Alexander paused. "I worked hard." Alexander's experiences on the farm colored her choice of her lifework. She attended college, received bachelor's and master's degrees in education, and never worked on a farm again. Farming was, for her, "very little pleasure. It was work!"[13]

Dola Glenn Aiken raised five hundred to eight hundred pullets (baby chickens) every spring during her years as a farm woman. She gathered about thirty dozen eggs per day, sorted and cleaned them, put the eggs into cases, and took them to the grocery store for sale every few days. This thriving chicken business had to be shut down in the 1950s after a federal law declared that grocery stores had to get their eggs from places where they were "graded and candled."[14] The farm, however, thrived in other areas. The business went into dairy production in 1944 and incorporated as Aiken Acres in 1973, raising milk cows and beef cattle.

Texas native Joyce Brooks recalled her childhood on a farm that also served as a ranch. She discussed the hard work that went into each day of her childhood:

> Daddy rarely hired extra help—the whole family participated in all the chores. We had about 500 acres of farm and ranch land, and daddy

13. Alexander, interview, September 2006.
14. Aiken, memoir, 1984.

> leased more to work. I did not mind the ranch work, in fact I liked it, but detested the field work which consisted of stacking hay bales, helping with the thrashing, pulling corn and picking cotton, all in the Texas heat. When I was 9 years old, I was in the cotton patch, and I had just picked up enough cotton to put in my sack to make a mattress. Then I laid down on it between those tall rows of cotton, and made a vow: What I want to do with my life is to travel the world and write a book about it. It took me 60 years to step on all seven continents, and write two books, but I never gave up!

Brooks knew that farmwork wasn't what she would choose to do with her life. The nine-year-old already knew that she would rather be somewhere else than in the field. Brooks also thought, at that early age, that there were no advantages to farm life. "I wanted to get away from the farm and travel," she explained.[15] But upon reflection, she could think of one advantage: the abundance of fresh food available on their successful spread. That abundance made a difference, particularly, she noted, during the war years.

Melvin Buhrkuhl wrote about his mother, in whom his father had complete confidence as his business partner. He recalled a season in the middle of harvest, when it emerged that the threshing crew—twenty-five men—would be arriving at their farm earlier than expected. Laura Buhrkuhl was given two hours to make a noon meal for the entire lot. "Mother met the challenge with a wood cook stove and home-canned food from our cellar," Buhrkuhl wrote. "The meal consisted of canned roast beef and gravy, vegetables and home-made cheese, butter and jam. [Laura had baked bread the day before.] All 25 men were satisfied with this meal, even though there was no pie or cake."[16] Buhrkuhl remembered that the entire family worked from daylight to dark six days a week.

The daily abundance of food, often preserved through the talents and labor of the farm woman, often was understood and related in the context of the work involved to obtain such abundance. Dorothy Fehrenbach was born in 1911, the youngest of ten children, and raised on a farm in Ohio. She recounted the production of wool from sheep kept on the farm and focused on the production of food. "We raised everything we ate on the farm: vegetables, fruit and all our meat. We had cows so we had milk, cream, butter, buttermilk, cottage cheese, and of

15. Brooks, letter to author, December 30, 2006.
16. Buhrkuhl, memoir, 1996.

course, we had chickens so we always had eggs," she wrote. Fehrenbach talked about selling the excess produce to grocers in Cincinnati; the family also raised hogs and sold them to processing plants in Cincinnati. Writing at age ninety-five, Dorothy lamented that she'd never bought a small farm as an adult. "There is nothing like those good fresh fruit and vegetables, and you don't have to worry about the poison sprays and the gases put on them. Our food is so contaminated with all these additives which they think it's OK but it's not."[17]

Helen Helder remembered in her 1992 memoir that her family worked together as a team to make the farm a success. "Sleep late—no way! That was unheard of!" she wrote. "Each member of the farm family had their own tasks to do as each day began, and we began the day together." She recalled the prescribed work roles, tasks for boys and girls, men and women, and in doing so stressed the notion that a successful farm depended on a successful family team. For Helder, assuring the success of that team fell to the woman who ran the household. Women also helped each other with the loneliness that could arise with their geographic isolation. Once she gave up teaching for housekeeping, Dola Aiken admitted to being lonely. "Glen worked long hours on his father's farm," she remembered. Her mother-in-law and sisters-in-law helped her pass the time with needle and craftwork. "We passed the time with piecing quilts, crocheting, and going places together. Lela taught me to crochet and she did beautiful work. To this day, I still crochet a lot."[18]

A Texas woman recalled that her mother ran the farm while her father worked in the oil fields. The heavier chores around the farm waited for her father to come home, and then the pair worked side by side to get everything accomplished. But her mother worked at a variety of tasks in addition to the management of the farm; she sewed all the family's clothes, taught Sunday school, acted as a Girl Scout leader and the PTA president, and helped with schoolwork. Elaine Friedrichsen, an Iowa farmer, recalls being a "farmer's wife" in the 1950s, with four children to raise. "I never had an 'off the farm' job," she wrote. "I had a big garden to tend, I canned some veggies (not as many as my mother did in the 30s and 40s), I raised chickens, ducks and geese; I butchered these for meat, kept hens for eggs." Friedrichsen reflected that her partnership with her husband included helping raise the cattle and hogs,

17. Fehrenbach, letter to author, January 25, 2006.
18. Helder, *In One Lifetime,* 7; Aiken, memoir, 1984.

milking cows, sewing children's clothes, putting up hay, and occasionally feeding big meals to farm crews of as many as eight men. "Farm wives are very busy people but very happy," she added. "We enjoyed going to dances, small town parades, etc; picnic with relatives, ball games among the men. We went to the small town church every Sunday. Life on the farm now is very different."[19]

These simple stories illustrate what farming magazines told readers: farm women worked hard, and the most successful farms depended upon farmers—both men and women—working hard together.

Farming in the Great Depression

The Depression years seem to have been as polarizing for those who lived through them as they appeared to be in the magazines. Some women who lived on farms during those years, particularly in the region known as the Dust Bowl—Kansas, Oklahoma, Nebraska—recalled daily struggles with dirt and drought. Those who wrote didn't downplay these problems, but it is also more than possible that some who lived through those years did not care to share or even recall what must have been a horrific period in many respects.

One Wisconsin woman looked back at farming during the Depression with a shudder: "When I think of those years growing up on the farm, I immediately think of hard work, dirty conditions and being cold. I was born in 1931 during the depression. We were very poor and those were such hard years it is almost beyond description." Another woman talked about using clean sheets to cover windows, even in the high heat of summer, to keep the dirt from blowing into the house. The sheets would be filthy within minutes of being put up. Many who did not own their own farms talked about multiple moves during those years, migrating from farm to farm as tenants before giving up and turning to the city.

Jean Jordan's story is typical. The Kansas native was a small girl in the early years of the Depression. She recounted move after move in response to changing conditions, as her parents' household shifted from farm to farm and relative to relative. Her father, the son of a farmer, didn't have his own land to work or enough money to start his own farm and had to rely on finding work with other farmers to survive.[20]

19. Friedrichsen, letter to author, January 15, 2007.
20. Jordan, interview, September 2006.

June Webb recalled both the comfortable days of her early childhood in the 1920s on a Nebraska farm and the later, difficult times of the Depression. Her father was one of thirteen children on a prosperous homestead where he and his family lived until Webb was in her early teens. "I think he and mom decided they kind of wanted to get out from underneath my grandfather's thumb; they kind of wanted a place of their own," she recalled. But the early 1930s were not good years in which to start a farm; land was cheap in the sand hills of Nebraska, but the drought made life difficult. "On the farm, we didn't have irrigation," Webb said. "When it rained, we would get out and stand in the rain, and run in the rain and say, 'Come down, oh Nebraska, come down.' The men would get out. We would get such a thrill when we got the rain." Economic conditions also made it difficult to get men to help with the farmwork; many had gone to the cities to try to find some kind of job. The story of Billie Hicks Parker is typical. She recounted her Depression childhood on a Louisiana cotton farm, detailing the poor economic conditions that drove her parents to give up farming. "Farmers were held in servitude," she wrote. "After paying your loan off, very little came home to family, those needing shoes, school clothes and supplies." After the family sold the farm and moved to a small town in northern Louisiana, where her father found work, each member of the family took a job to maintain the whole.[21]

But the Depression didn't bring desperate times for everyone. Some who did own their farms talked about tightening budgets but remembered always having food to eat and clothes to wear. Joyce Kollars remembered the farm being the best place to be during those years. "We were very poor, but we always had plenty of cream, milk, eggs, meat and canned vegetables from the garden. We never were hungry." Born in 1931, Kollars was the oldest of ten children, and it fell to her and her sister to wash clothes by hand every Saturday, boiling the water in big copper pans. Once the clothes were clean, they were hung out to dry, regardless of the season. The family made its own soap and hauled seemingly endless supplies of wood and corncobs to heat the house. "Each summer, we older girls had to go help our aunts," she recalled. "From the time I was six till I was eighteen, I went to help. I got very homesick and hated to go, but our family had older girls and we were expected to help when we could. I would have to cook for the thrashers,

21. Webb, interview, September 2006; Parker, letter to author, February 15, 2007.

help with newborn babies, and clean all summer long."[22] The hardships of the labor involved in surviving, however, led her to open the memoir with: "Those were such hard years it is almost beyond description."

Joyce Brooks was born in 1933, "just as the depression was kinda ending." She was seven years older than her only sibling, a brother, and that meant having to help her father with all the chores on the farm. "We were not poor—but certainly not rich!" Brooks noted. Iowa native Elaine Friedrichsen grew up during the Depression years on her family's farm and, when she wrote in January 2007, still lived on her own farm. Life, she said, was never boring on the farm. She particularly loved to work with the animals and looked back with a nostalgic fondness on a childhood spent helping with myriad farm tasks.[23]

Vi Melton, in recalling her early childhood in the 1930s, observed that barter often served as well as cash in getting small luxuries like the *Farm Journal*. Her mother traded two hens for their two-year subscription. "We were very poor," Melton remembered, adding in parentheses that it took her years to see that. "But so was almost everyone else." Living in Kansas's Dust Bowl was a trial. "The dust bowl days were anything but pleasant," Melton recalled.

> Mama would drop wet sheets over our bodies from the head to the feet on the bedsteads [at night], and in the morning, they were muddy.
>
> The dirt was so deep in places, the cows would walk from pasture to pasture cause the posts and fences were buried.
>
> We had no plumbing, telephone or electricity, so we did our homework by kerosene lantern light. It was a rough time for the family, but somehow, Dad and Mom kept us warm and not hungry. We always ate the same things. But not knowing any better, we accepted it.[24]

Melton left home at fifteen to live with her married older sister.

Dola Aiken graduated from high school in 1928. She took the test required to become a schoolteacher and passed it, teaching her first term of school in 1928. She recalled that in her home state of Kansas in those years, married women were not allowed to teach school. When

22. Kollars, memoir, 2007.

23. Brooks, letter to author, December 30, 2006; Friedrichsen, letter to author, January 15, 2007.

24. Melton, letter to author, February 11, 2007.

the stock market crashed in 1929, times were sufficiently hard that she put off marrying Glen Aiken until 1934 in order to keep her job. Even so, when the couple married in the summer of 1934, they opted to elope and keep their marriage secret in order for Dola to continue teaching through the spring of 1935.[25] The ingenuity and secretiveness required to maintain an income in years when money was hard to come by are characteristic of this era. As her daughter-in-law wrote, this particular part of family history seemed terribly romantic to Dola's descendants.

The key problem facing those who migrated appeared to be that they did not own any land themselves. If a family owned its own farm, free and clear, times were no tougher than usual. Those who had to rely on relatives, friends, or jobs off the farm had a difficult time making ends meet, and they were forced to move to find better living conditions. Everybody struggled, but the degree of struggle varied.

Doing Without

A common thread running through the conversations was that life demanded sacrifices, and families were expected to "do without" the conveniences of "modern living" when necessary. In many rural communities, basics such as electricity were late to arrive, and money was unavailable to provide some conveniences. For example, as Minnesota native Allien Ahlman recalled, writing in 2007, the farm home she shared with her husband for fifty-two years was heated with wood until 2003, and in her first years on the farm during the 1950s, she had no running water in the house she shared with her in-laws. "No hot water, no bathroom indoors. Pump water from a cistern under the kitchen. Rain water of course. Nothing like it. Gravity from a faucet for drinking water. Then in 1959 his dad remodeled the old house. Then is when we had the wood furnace, cemented floor in the basement, hot water heater, full bathroom, wood floors, I was in heaven," she said in her letter. "Our last son was the only one born after the house was remodeled. Up until three years ago I still used a ringer-type washing machine."[26]

Dola Aiken's first child was born in 1936, "at high noon," on their farm. The baby, a girl, was ill, dirtying multiple diapers that required water to wash, and the farm's well had run dry. With no indoor plumbing, a "cross" baby, no water or air-conditioning, it was a "bad summer"

25. Aiken, memoir, 1984.
26. Ahlman, letter to author, February 25, 2007.

for Dola. "I thought I had made a bad trade from school teaching to motherhood," she recalled. With winter and weather changes, the baby settled down, and Dola adjusted, learning to enjoy her new role as wife and mother.[27]

Dola got her first Servel Electrolux refrigerator in early 1941, and "we had refrigeration without setting in the block of ice that was brought from town," she wrote. "I don't think I have ever appreciated an appliance more than this one." Dorothy Fehrenbach recalled getting the family's first radio when she was twelve, in 1923, and a five-party telephone line. "If someone else was using it, you had to wait," she remembered. Helen Helder described the party line to her farm as essential; when it arrived, it took away some of the loneliness of stormy winter days, she recalled. Olivia Merryman was raised on her parents' Mississippi farm. "Had no electricity til I was about 14, so we used kerosene lamps to do homework," she reported. But her family was well enough off to be subscribers both to *Farm Journal* and to *Progressive Farmer.* "I was a teen before we got a radio. . . . Saw TV for first time on my senior class trip to New Orleans in May of 1951. We had no TV at home, or even a telephone." Kathryn Severs said her family never had any "modern" things in the house she grew up in, "unless you call the old Party line Telephone 'modern.' My parents didn't get electricity until I left home, to work, at age 18. Then REA came through the country with 'high' lines."[28]

This sense of doing without also extended to travel. Many women recounted the use of buggies, horses, or their own two feet to get from one place to another, and several mentioned that women who were expecting babies rarely left the farm, in part because the existing modes of travel were considered too rough for women to endure if it wasn't necessary. Dola Aiken noted that the activities that did draw people away from their homes were events such as the county fair. Her own memoir also told about walking to school through the meadows and pastures of prairie grass that would be higher than a small girl's head. "Each September before school started, Dad would mow a path across the meadow and pasture with his horse-drawn mower so I would not get lost walking to and from school," Dola remembered. The family got its first car in 1924, a Model T Ford.[29]

27. Aiken, memoir, 1984.

28. Ibid.; Fehrenbach, letter to author, January 25, 2007; Helder, *In One Lifetime,* 56; Merryman, letter to author, March 19, 2007; Severs, letter to author, January 4, 2007.

29. Dola Glenn Aiken, memoir, 1984.

Perceptions of the Urban World

Many women recounted the advantages that city life could have afforded the farm woman, including ready access to social activities and goods. But more often than not, women said they'd prefer not to live in an urban area, offering perceptions of the city as dangerous and overcrowded.

For South Dakota native Lois Laferriere, the old phrase "a nice place to visit but I wouldn't want to live there" applied to any community of ten thousand or more people. "City living was something far away," she wrote. Louisiana native Billie Hicks Parker viewed the cities as places of "moral breakdown." "I have never lived in a city. Hope never to. The small little towns with country people [are] what keeps our U.S.A. from going 'overboard,'" she wrote. "There is heart, willingness to help; a neighbor, anyone needing help." Vera Scott said she'd never lived in the city; her farm home, on which she'd retired at the time of her writing, gave her everything she'd want.[30]

Yet, while most wouldn't choose to live in the city, some did choose not to live on a farm. "When I was growing up, I said I'd never live on a farm (and I haven't) but the older I've gotten, the fonder I've gotten of farm living," Kathryn Severs related. Phyllis Spade recalled taking her homemade bread sandwich to school in the 1940s. "I never had a nice neat slice of bread, and I took my sandwiches to school with this misshapen bread. And I was so ashamed of it, because all of the girls from town had boughten bread and they were nice and neat, and here were my misshapen sandwiches." Spade's mother made her bread in a large square pan, in three loaves that touched each other, so that the middle loaf rose tall and skinny, while the side loaves were apt to spread. Her school lunch contained this homemade bread with home-cured ham, roast beef, or chicken, and "wonderful food." But Spade continued to envy the town girls their uniform slices of bread and bologna. "We never bought bologna," she recounted. "My mother was sure it wasn't fit to eat."[31]

30. Laferriere, letter to author, January 4, 2007; Parker, letter to author, February 15, 2007; Scott, letter to author, February 18, 2007.

31. Severs, letter to author, January 4, 2007; Spade, personal interview, September 11, 2006.

This kind of subtle envy appeared to cut both ways. Some women told of their town friends wanting to learn to milk cows, or ride horses, or play and run in the pastures, while the farm girls and women wanted access to some of the convenience foods and leisure activities available in town. For those women who viewed the city as offering an easier life, the decision to leave the farm was simple. City living offered opportunities for those women who wanted them, and the chief opportunity appeared to be education. Nearly all the women who talked about leaving the farm at a young age said they did so either to marry or to go to school. The primary professions into which women were channeled included nursing, education, and business. June Webb, for example, went to business school, then joined the WAVES during the Second World War.

Others moved to town because they had no choice. Spade, for example, married a young man from a neighboring farm in 1947. "By that time, a young couple couldn't hardly start into farming; they couldn't afford to set up," she said. "My parents weren't ready to give up the farm, and he was not enamoured by the farm work, and it just happened. We didn't deliberately leave the farm; it was just the way it was."[32]

32. Spade, personal interview, September 11, 2006.

7
Lives in Transition

"My view of city life was WOW!" wrote Kathleen Gilsdorf from Columbus, Nebraska.

> You could make waffles on an electric iron. We could walk on side walks and never need overshoes or carry mud into the house.
>
> I don't remember ever wanting to live in town. I loved horses and walking a mile to bring cows in to milk. We milked [more than] 25 cows by hand day and night. I had close friends living in town. We went to Catholic school, so we were in town every day. Five days for school, Saturday night for groceries and selling eggs and cream, and Sunday for Mass.
>
> I felt more that my friends envied me. They rode bikes five miles to our farm to see us separate milk for cream and to ride in the wagon that my Dad pulled with horses.
>
> Now that I live in the city I realize what an easy time the women in town had when it came to cleaning and cooking, but also what a challenge they faced to prepare meals. We always had meat, milk, cream, eggs, fruit from our apple orchard and vegetables from a large garden. When sugar, coffee, shoes [and such] were rationed during World War II we exchanged stamps with friends in town. We always had plenty of sugar and coffee, but we needed shoes.
>
> We had a battery radio that we used in evening for a couple hours so it would not lose its charge. We needed it for market reports. We always got *Capper's Weekly.* It had an assortment of articles, recipes, patterns, jokes and news. We really got the news of the week on Saturday night in town. We caught up on everything. I remember we heard about Pearl Harbor in Mass. Father announced it in Mass. That is the same way we learned that one of the young men in our parish had been killed.
>
> We were more concerned with marketprices and local happenings. After the war started, it was entirely different.[1]

Kathleen's story touches on the complexity of what it meant to be a farm woman in America between 1910 and 1960. That pivotal fifty

1. Gilsdorf, letter to author, May 15, 2007.

years encompassed a variety of changes in the American cultural landscape that affected, and perhaps drove, a population shift that brought a significant number of rural citizens into urban areas. Farming in 1910 looked different from farming in 1960, and those who survived the changes on the farm with their land holdings intact also became farm life's biggest boosters. Those who were forced to leave the farm in order to survive looked back with mixed feelings—nostalgia for a simpler form of country life, abundant in food, mixed with remembrances of hard work and the struggle required to survive. That struggle, keenly apparent in interviews and correspondence with women raised on farms or running farms during those fifty years, is less apparent in magazines targeted to farm families during that period.

This research started with my remembrance of my grandmother, Elsie Coen Mattson, in her farmhouse kitchen. It came out of a sense that the dominant construction of farm women as victims, as symbolized by the Dorothea Lange image of the migrant mother, Florence Thompson, was not altogether accurate. I recognized something of that woman, but my own lived experiences in a family with close farming ties in northern Wisconsin had taught me something very different: farm women were to be respected. As I struggled to understand the differences between urban or mainstream perceptions and my own lived perceptions, this research was born.

I wanted to know which was the more accurate image: farm woman as victim, or farm woman as a respected part of the business of farming. The farming and mainstream magazines I studied showed me that the second image, that of the farm woman as respected in the business of farming, was the more socially accepted one within the farming community. Farm women themselves, though, told me that while this was certainly true, particularly among middle-class landowning farmers, the role of a respected farm woman was much more complicated than the media studied for this research would suggest. None of the women who talked to or corresponded with me could be construed as passive; each made her choice and lived with her decision. But it was clear that each also knew that farming was a business, and a choice to remain on the farm or to leave it was a choice between one career and the potential for a different one. Early on in those fifty years, for a woman who wanted a career in business, farming was a more sensible choice than working in the limited number of positions available to women off the farm during that period.

But what of the women who didn't perceive the choice? The undercurrent to the stories told by farm women and written in farming magazines suggested that farmers as a group, both men and women, recognized the hardships that occurred with a business that depended on weather and a host of economic factors for its success. The fact that the survival of the business and the survival of the family as a unit were closely linked cannot be overlooked. For some women, raised on farms and married off as teens, there may not have been a good alternative, given that the terms were this: work hard on a farm and depend on yourself to survive, or face the uncertainty and limited job choices available in a city, where a paycheck depends on someone else's goodwill. Farming, and the work of farms, was what they knew and were comfortable with. It took a strong woman to decide to leave that comfort zone to carve out another kind of life in an urban area, to seek an education and pursue a different kind of career. It took an equally strong woman to stay on the farm, manage the business, home, and family, and face the challenges of independent survival.

Fifty Years of Media Constructions

The constructions of farm women in mainstream and farming magazines changed little over fifty years. Farm women were consistently presented as vital and necessary to the business of farming. They were respected for their common sense and practicality and for their brains and entrepreneurial spirit. These qualities led some to view farm women as perhaps more deserving of the vote than their urban counterparts. Yet their roles on farms, and the very centrality of their existence to the farm, home, and business, kept farm women from participating in politics to a large degree. Citizenship appears to have meant exercising the right to vote, expressing their opinions through mass media, taking active roles in farming organizations, and agitating for needed educational opportunities and programs directed toward the farm home. Because farm women made up a significant part of the American population and still are the only group of women consistently part of the history of a major American industry, what they did surely had an impact.

As noted in the Introduction, according to the U.S. Census Bureau, in 1910, more than 32 million people in the United States lived on 6.3 million farms, which at the time was nearly 35 percent of the U.S. population. In 1960, 13.5 million people lived on 3.7 million farms, comprising 7.5 percent of the U.S. population. Assuming at least one farm woman per farm household, there were more than six million farm women in 1910 and almost four million farm women in 1960. Additionally, an average of 5.2 people—a farm family unit—lived on an American farm in 1910, while an average of 3.6 people lived on an American farm in 1960, a decline that may have roots in the mechanization of farm labor. In 1960, the number of people living on farms was half what it had been in 1910; but, assuming farming still constituted a business conducted by a man and a woman farmer in partnership, the number of farm women did not decline as drastically. This indicates a kind of stability in a declining way of life centered on farm women, if only symbolically. Contrary to scholarship suggesting that farm women needed prodding to change their social position and business opportunities, the women seen in the farm periodicals and in farm women's writing seem to have been deeply absorbed in business opportunities and content with their social position.

In farm magazines, women were constructed as central to the running of the farm business. They kept accounts, ran the dairy and poultry operations, produced garden produce for sale and for consumption, managed a household of varied family members, including children and sometimes parents and grandparents, and worked unceasingly to keep up with it all. Farm women were depicted as needing labor-saving and time-saving devices to help them manage the amount of work demanded of them; they were depicted as needing varied educational opportunities, both for personal enrichment and for business advancement. Farm women were depicted as capable, competent, and smart businesswomen whose individual successes were models for farm progress, particularly in the early years covered by this research. Farm women were constructed in farm magazines as worthy of the vote; their business interests and prowess helped to keep them informed about civic issues. As a function of their citizenship, farm women were urged to stay on the farms in their capacities as producers of food, especially during the years of the two world wars. The sources studied implied that it was farm women's duty as informed citizens to work on the farm and to produce food. They also suggested that citizenship for farm women meant agitating for national legislation on behalf of farm business and farm home issues.

In mainstream magazines, farm women were constructed as practical and wise, keepers of the public trust and American values, and rich in common sense, if not in actual cash. This construction was seen most prominently in *Ladies' Home Journal.* Farm women were depicted as unable to participate in city leisure pursuits. This portrayal did not change significantly across issues studied from 1910 to 1960, and perhaps because of this inability to pursue city leisure or interact with a growing urban consumer culture, farm women were depicted as oddities at the end of this period.

No discussion of farm women was seen in *Good Housekeeping* issues read. Farming was alluded to only in the context of farm methods and pricing that ultimately resulted in higher prices for consumers. In the *Saturday Evening Post* issues read, farm women were constructed as businesspeople. The content portrays farm women as "unfeminine," plain, and interested only in practical pursuits. On the whole, farm women's work is invisible in the women's magazines, and no clear construction of farm women as farmers was found.

The issues read encouraged farm women—and all women—as citizens to exercise their right to vote and agitate for change. The choice of issues for which women might most capably agitate differed from publication to publication, but women were most often encouraged to agitate for traditionally domestic issues—maternal and child health, public health, education, and public safety. Farm women discussed these issues publicly and helped to raise awareness among others, especially about child safety on farms.

The greatest change identifiable in these constructions over time is in mainstream magazines, which in 1910 gave significant attention to farming and farm women's issues but by 1960 rarely mentioned farm women. In the mainstream magazines, women's voices were absent in the years immediately following World War II. Readers' letters were not seen in the *Good Housekeeping* issues read, for example. From depicting women as politically active, content went to ignoring women's views.

But farm magazines depicted women as strong and as central to the culture and especially the farm community throughout the period under study. The farm magazine editors provided space for women to air grievances, problems, and triumphs and to reach out to each other. Women's discussions in the columns included politics.

Fifty Years of Farm Women Journalists

In responding to my request for information, some women wrote back asking how much I'd pay for their stories. Hearing the answer—which was "nothing"—all but one of those women declined to participate in the work. For most farm women journalists, writing for pay was a way to supplement the family income, so they surely knew what would sell—and stories about overworked and overburdened farm women were not what would sell to the farming magazines.

Still, their writing was valuable for the peek it yielded into their lives. Farm women writers constructed farm women as capable women who worked unceasingly, but were content, even happy, as farmers. Farm women writers discussed farm women as important to the farm home, and the farm home as important to the business. These women expected to be respected for their skills as homemakers and as farmers, and they expected that their reputations as farmers preceded them in the marketplace.

However, farm women writers also discussed farm women as overworked, underpaid, and lacking in the respect they deserved from male farmers. The farm women who connected with each other via letters to the editors acted as a collective sounding board. Many letters detailed measures used to manipulate men farmers into helping women with their work. In that sense, women constructed farm women as clever members of a resistance group against a dominant patriarchal system; in the process, they reinforced their centrality to the success of the farming business.

As citizens, farm women were constructed by farm women writers as active in farming and women's organizations that agitated for causes, such as education for rural children, woman suffrage, and aid for the farm home. These writers also constructed farm women as focusing on the uniqueness of their individual situations while urging each other to act collectively for change within their communities. Activism was constructed as a function of citizenship not easily filled by married farm women with small children. Participation in politics and other movements was easier for older married women whose family demands had lessened, or for single farm girls who did not have such family commitments. No significant change in these constructions over time was seen. The farm women's writing stressed the farm home as central to the farm business and farm women as vital to the success of the farming business, even as they discussed the lack of educational opportunities for farm women. And they depicted farm women as innovative individuals who could easily find solutions to everyday problems and who could take over any part of the farm business at a moment's notice. Farm women journalists also called farm women worthy of suffrage and careers in public service, in part because of their very capabilities. They discussed farm women as a group as wise and practical. However, farm women journalists also constructed farm women as overworked and needing labor-saving devices, rest, and leisure. These same women journalists discussed strategies for manipulating men farmers into providing the kinds of help and support women needed in their varied roles on farms. These farm women journalists suggested ways to resist and change conventional gender norms while supporting farm women's needs in their homes and in the public sphere.

By the end of the period under study, the farm community had been marginalized in mainstream sources read. Farm women writers also constructed farm women as in need of rest and educational opportunities. Farm women also were portrayed by farm women journalists as resisting patriarchal culture through their manipulation of husbands to get their needs met. Farm women may have been more inclined toward collective action than farm men; at least, the magazines studied showed that they readily connected with each other, perhaps to find way to lighten their workloads, but more likely to maintain the thriving community of interest that was facilitated by the media they chose to read and contribute to.

One slight change over time was that more mechanization and labor-saving devices became available, with the result that more farm women were depicted as able to focus on the farm home. The lack of educational opportunities for farm women and children, a significant issue early in the period under study, was addressed over time through university programs that implemented distance-learning courses as early as 1915. The farm magazines offered at-home self-improvement courses, for a fee, and fostered rural women's clubs as a means of helping women advance their educations. Some women wrote in the later years of this period about their college experiences.

The social and geographic isolation of farm women seen in magazine content from the early years was seen in magazine issues from the later years as well. In the 1950s, this isolation was depicted as an asset. The farm was a place of relative safety in an unsafe world under the threat of nuclear annihilation, a place that would soothe the spirits of soldiers returning from World War II and Korea, a haven for women as well as for men. This construction fits with other historians' observations that containment in the home seemed the way American culture handled these threats in the post–World War II period.

Talking to Farm Women: Fifty Years of Remembrance

"She rose at dawn with the rest of the family, even after caring for sick ones at night or giving the babies their night feedings," Helen Helder wrote. "She planned the food and clothing for her family, pinched pennies to accommodate priorities, and encouraged her husband in his efforts. The farm wife was indeed the helpmate and soul mate of each successful farmer."[2] Reflecting on her own experiences and beliefs as a farm women, Helder articulated the construction of farm women that appeared not only in magazines but also in interviews and correspondence with women who lived on farms during the period under study.

One of the remarkable things that arose from the oral history portion of this research was how similar women's experiences were from geographic region to geographic region. While the business of farming varies depending on a region's resources—Kansas farmers raise wheat, for example, while farmers in the South raise warm-weather crops like cotton—the women who wrote from these diverse regions shared similar stories. Over and over again, these women detailed the tremendous amount of work that went into being a farm woman. Although their specific duties varied, the women all took responsibility for running the farm home, raising children, gardening, and dealing with livestock—particularly chickens and other poultry. Some gave up careers in teaching, nursing, or the military to take their jobs as farmers; others, raised in the life, embraced it without a backward glance. Still others, raised in farm homes, opted out of a career in farming.

Economic class divisions also become apparent as the stories are read as a collective whole. Some farms survived the Depression more or less intact, with family members contributing to the overall success of the farm. Others did not. The key seems to have been landownership. Those who owned their own land outright before the crash appeared to be able to stick with farming through the rough drought years. Migration occurred when families did not own the land they worked. The migrants were second or third sons or daughters who did not inherit the family farms and thus were cast out to find their own way, or tenant farmers struggling already to eke a living from land they did not own.

2. Helder, *In One Lifetime,* 8.

There was solidarity evident in the struggle with the land, but it was equally evident that the constructions of farming, and farm women, offered in the national farming magazines applied only to those who could afford to farm.

Fifty Years of Perception: The Urban versus Rural Divide

The research also reveals a clear and expanding gap between rural and urban constructions of farm women and farm life. The widening of the gap can be seen in how farm women were constructed in comparison to urban women over time.

For their part, urban women constructed farm women as plain, unsophisticated, and even a marginalized "other" in American culture. As noted in Chapter 3, "The Country Contributor" wrote in 1915 of the farm woman that she was "the typification of the thing America needs more than it needs any other thing."[3] This construction correlates with the increasing urbanization shown by the U.S. Census Bureau figures. America was becoming a consumer society; hence, one is tempted to see the construction as a "message" to farm women to consume more of the fashions and modern-day products advertised—especially in mainstream magazines in which the construction is particularly marked.

Farm periodicals and farm women also constructed farm women as different from their urban counterparts. They presented farm women as virtually the "backbone" of one form of American business and economy. These women appear as hard-working, sturdy, resilient, reliable, and wise; indeed, today's reader gets an impression from these sources that farm women would know what to do and could shoulder the task in any crisis. Constructions of urban women were less defined in farm women's writings, but today's reader gathers the impression that farm women viewed them as "soft" and less prepared for life's challenges.

The idea of farm women as big-business women, set in contrast to city women, who were constructed as knowing little about their husbands' work and doing less of their own, epitomizes this rural-urban gap. The striking finding regarding the business role of farm women is best exemplified, as we have seen, by the notice given to it by "experts" in home

3. "A Plain Country Woman," *Ladies' Home Journal*, November 1915, 30.

economics and agriculture. The daughters of those farm women who stayed on the farm likely carried with them what their mothers modeled—deep involvement with the farm business and a clearly defined role in a significant subculture (the farm culture) of American society. At least, this is suggested by the fact that the constructions of farm women seen in farm periodicals and in farm women's writings in the 1910s were much like those seen in the 1950s.

This persisting role of farm women likely affected the thinking of the generations they raised, generations that fought for the second wave of the feminist movement in the 1960s. Additionally, it appears that the focus on the independence of farmers, tied to the agrarian ideal of Thomas Jefferson and reinforced by the economic conditions of farming that enforced hard work as necessary to survival, demonstrates a kind of political conservatism that may have affected the generations of young people raised on farms that headed to the city. It is possible that these agrarian values, brought to the city, may partially account for a political shift in the American working class from liberal to conservative in the years after the period under study here. The farm women seen and "heard" through this research were mothers of at least three generations that came of age before the end of the twentieth century. It seems highly likely that what they modeled politically as citizens as well as what they modeled as women shaped the political views of those generations.

Community-Building Function of Media

It is evident that mass media functioned to maintain and build communities whose members were geographically widespread, as farm women used magazines to connect with each other. While this function has received comparatively little study from historians, the burgeoning area of computer-mediated communication offers some explanation for the phenomenon revealed here.

The use of the farming magazines as community-building media seems similar to the ways people today use Internet social networking sites. The recent introduction of the Internet and the World Wide Web has sparked research into computer-mediated communication, which by its nature allows communication over great distances and at great speeds. In one sense, farm women's use of magazines to foster communication with other farm women seems to have set a precedent for today's use of the Web for connecting with others at distances.

The use of such media for community-building makes evident the process of negotiating messages (and making meaning) that scholars have discussed but rarely illustrated. That is, it is clear that the professionals who produced these media created a reality of farm life, and it is also clear that this reality was then reshaped by audience members during their use of the medium as a mechanism for interpersonal communication.

Marked differences were seen between constructions of farm women in mainstream and farming magazines. The fact that the differences appear particularly in the 1930s and beyond may reflect a cultural shift afoot in American values—or at least a divergence that was sharpening distinctions between agrarian and urban subcultures. One key difference between the mainstream and farming publications is the number of letters and reader-writer contributors to farming magazines. These contributors were not passively receiving messages that brought them someone else's constructions of them. They were actively using the medium for community building and thereby shaping their own realities. That active role in self-constructions likely contributed to the stability of the constructions of farm women in the farm magazines over time. The fact that those constructions remained stable while constructions in mainstream magazines fluctuated suggests that media that provide a community-building function may play a significant role in some kinds of cultural stability. That is, the reader-writer/editor relationship in media where each is treated as a valued contributor may aid in facilitating a stable, communal culture. In any event, audience input seems essential to that stability.

Research here also shows that, as farming culture became increasingly marginalized by mainstream culture, audiences for farming magazines could read material that consistently constructed farming culture in opposition to mainstream (urban) culture. This, in effect, provides more evidence of competing constructions of "reality." What are the implications for theories of mass culture when distinct subcultures construct themselves in ways that are at odds with a dominant culture? Research for this work suggests that "mass culture" is a myth; competing subcultures are constantly constructing realities independent of a dominant culture. It also suggests that the community-building function of media has been at play for far longer than computer-mediated communication has been in existence.

Food for Thought

The research reported here just begins to scratch the surface of these issues, but it points out the work about the place of farm women in American culture that needs to be done. These women were more than farmer's wives. That farm women had an impact in American history is certain. The depth and dimensions of that impact remain to be studied.

Appendix
Magazine Issues Read

Country Gentleman (Philadelphia: Curtis Publishing Co.): 75:2971 (January 6, 1910); 75:2972 (January 13, 1910); 75:2973 (January 20, 1910); 75:2984 (April 7, 1910); 75:2985 (April 14, 1910); 75:2986 (April 21, 1910); 75:2997 (July 7, 1910); 75:2998 (July 14, 1910); 75:2999 (July 21, 1910); 75:3010 (October 6, 1910); 75:3011 (October 13, 1910); 75:3012 (October 20, 1910); 80:6 (February 6, 1915); 80:7 (February 13, 1915); 80:8 (February 20, 1915); 80:18 (May 1, 1915); 80:19 (May 8, 1915); 80:20 (May 15, 1915); 80:32 (August 7, 1915); 80:33 (August 14, 1915); 80:34 (August 21, 1915); 80:45 (November 6, 1915); 80:46 (November 13, 1915); 80:47 (November 20, 1915); 85:10 (March 6, 1920); 85:11 (March 13, 1920); 85:12 (March 20, 1920); 85:23 (June 5, 1920); 85:24 (June 12, 1920); 85:25 (June 19, 1920); 85:36 (September 4, 1920); 85:37 (September 11, 1920); 85:38 (September 18, 1920); 85:49 (December 4, 1920); 85:50 (December 11, 1920); 85:51 (December 18, 1920); 90:1 (January 3, 1925); 90:2 (January 10, 1925); 90:3 (January 17, 1925); 90:14 (April 4, 1925); 90:15 (April 11, 1925); 90:16 (April 18, 1925); 90:27 (July 4, 1925); 90:28 (July 11, 1925); 90:29 (July 18, 1925); 90:36 (October 1925); 95:2 (February 1930); 95:5 (May 1930); 95:8 (August 1930); 95:11 (November 1930); 105:3 (March 1935); 105:6 (June 1935); 105:9 (September 1935); 105:12 (December 1935); 110:1 (January 1940); 110:4 (April 1940); 110:7 (July 1940); 110:10 (October 1940); 115:2 (February 1945); 115:5 (May 1945); 115:8 (August 1945); 115:11 (November 1945); 120:3 (March 1950); 120:6 (June 1950); 120:9 (September 1950); 120:12 (December 1950); (*Better Living*) 125:1 (January 1955); (*Better Living*) 125:4 (April 1955); (*Better Living*) 125:7 (July 1955).

The Farmer's Wife (St. Paul: Webb Publishing Co.): 15:3 (March 1910);[1]

1. Volume numbers are irregular, with volumes 15 and 16 repeating. Refer to the date for the specific issue.

15:6 (June 1910); 15:9 (September 1910); 15:12 (December 1910); 16:1 (January 1911); 16:4 (April 1911); 16:7 (July 1911); 16:10 (October 1911); 15:2 (February 1912); 15:5 (May 1912); 15:8 (August 1912); 15:11 (November 1912); 16:3 (March 1913); 16:6 (June 1913); 16:9 (September 1913); 16:12 (December 1913); 17:1 (January 1914); 17:4 (April 1914); 17:7 (July 1914); 17:10 (October 1914); 18:2 (February 1915); 18:5 (May 1915); 18:8 (August 1915); 18:11 (November 1915); 19:3 (March 1916); 19:6 (June 1916); 19:9 (September 1916); 19:12 (December 1916); 20:1 (January 1917); 20:4 (April 1917); 20:7 (July 1917); 20:10 (October 1917); 21:2 (February 1918); 21:5 (May 1918); 21:8 (August 1918); 21:11 (November 1918); 22:3 (March 1919); 22:6 (June 1919); 22:9 (September 1919); 22:12 (December 1919); 23:1 (January 1920); 23:4 (April 1920); 23:7 (July 1920); 23:10 (October 1920); 24:2 (February 1921); 24:5 (May 1921); 24:8 (August 1921); 24:11 (November 1921); 25:3 (March 1922); 25:6 (June 1922); 25:9 (September 1922); 25:12 (December 1922); 26:1 (January 1923); 26:4 (April 1923); 26:7 (July 1923); 26:10 (October 1923); 27:2 (February 1924); 27:5 (May 1924); 27:8 (August 1924); 27:11 (November 1924); 26:3 (March 1925); 26:6 (June 1925); 26:9 (September 1925); 26:12 (December 1925); 27:1 (January 1926); 27:4 (April 1926); 27:7 (July 1926); 27:10 (October 1926); 33:2 (February 1930); 33:5 (May 1930); 33:8 (August 1930); 33:11 (November 1930); 38:1 (January 1935); 38:3 (March 1935); 38:6 (June 1935); 38:9 (September 1935); 38:12 (December 1935).[2]

Farm Journal (Philadelphia: Wilmer Atkinson Co.): 34:3 (March 1910); 34:6 (June 1910); 34:9 (September 1910); 34:12 (December 1910); 39:2 (February 1915); 39:5 (May 1915); 39:8 (August 1915); 39:11 (November 1915); 44:1 (January 1920); 44:4 (April 1920); 44:7 (July 1920); 44:10 (October 1920); 49:2 (February 1925); 49:5 (May 1925); 49:8 (August 1925); 49:11 (November 1925); 54:3 (March 1930); 54:6 (June 1930); 54:9 (September 1930); 54:12 (December 1930); 59:1 (January 1935); 59:4 (April 1935); 59:7 (July 1935); 59:10 (October 1935); 64:1 (January 1940); 64:4 (April 1940); 64:7 (July 1940); 64:10 (October 1940); 69:3 (March 1945); 69:6 (June 1945); 69:9 (September 1945); 69:12 (December 1945); 74:2 (February

2. Issues of *The Farmer's Wife* after December 1935 were bound into the back of *Farm Journal;* thus, notes referring to *The Farmer's Wife* after 1935 are referring to that issue of the *Farm Journal* in which *The Farmer's Wife* appeared.

1950); 74:5 (May 1950); 74:8 (August 1950); 74:11 (November 1950); 79:1 (January 1955); 79:4 (April 1955); 79:7 (July 1955); 79:10 (October 1955); 80:2 (February 1956); 80:5 (May 1956); 80:8 (August 1956); 80:11 (November 1956); 81:3 (March 1957); 81:6 (June 1957); 81:9 (September 1957); 81:12 (December 1957); 82:1 (January 1958); 82:4 (April 1958); 82:7 (July 1958); 82:10 (October 1958); 83:2 (February 1959); 83:5 (May 1959); 83:8 (August 1959); 83:11 (November 1959); 84:1 (January 1960); 84:2 (February 1960); 84:3 (March 1960); 84:4 (April 1960); 84:5 (May 1960); 84:6 (June 1960); 84:7 (July 1960); 84:8 (August 1960); 84:9 (September 1960); 84:10 (October 1960); 84:11 (November 1960); 84:12 (December 1960); 85:1 (January 1961); 85:12 (December 1961); 86:1 (January 1962); 86:12 (December 1962).

Good Housekeeping (New York: International Magazine Co.): 50:1 (January 1910); 50:4 (April 1910); 51:1 (July 1910); 51:4 (October 1910); 60:2 (February 1915); 60:5 (May 1915); 61:2 (August 1915); 61:5 (November 1915); 70:3 (March 1920); 70:6 (June 1920); 71:3 (September 1920); 71:6 (December 1920); 80:1 (January 1925); 80:4 (April 1925); 81:1 (July 1925); 81:4 (October 1925); 90:2 (February 1930); 90:5 (May 1930); 91:2 (August 1930); 91:5 (November 1930); 100:3 (March 1935); 100:6 (June 1935); 101:3 (September 1935); 101:6 (December 1935); 110:1 (January 1940); 110:4 (April 1940); 111:1 (July 1940); 111:4 (October 1940); 120:2 (February 1945); 120:5 (May 1945); 121:2 (August 1945); 121:5 (November 1945); 130:3 (March 1950); 130:6 (June 1950); 131:3 (September 1950); 131:6 (December 1950); 140:1 (January 1955); 140:4 (April 1955); 145:1 (July 1955); 141:4 (October 1955); 150:2 (February 1960); 150:5 (May 1960); 151:1 (July 1960); 151:5 (November 1960).

Ladies' Home Journal (Philadelphia: Curtis Publishing Co.): 27:2 (January 1910);[3] 27:5 (April 1910); 27:8 (July 1910); 27:13 (October 1910); 32:2 (February 1915); 32:5 (May 1915); 32:8 (August 1915); 32:11 (November 1915); 37:3 (March 1920); 37:6 (June 1920); 37:9 (September 1920); 37:12 (December 1920); 42:1 (January 1925); 42:4 (April 1925); 42:7 (July 1925); 42:10 (October 1925); 47:2 (February 1930); 47:5 (May 1930); 47:8 (August 1930); 47:11 (November 1930); 52:3 (March 1935); 52:6 (June 1935); 52:9 (September 1935);

3. Some volume and issue numbers are irregular. Refer to the date for the specific issue.

52:12 (December 1935); 57:1 (January 1940); 57:4 (April 1940); 57:7 (July 1940); 57:10 (October 1940); 62:2 (February 1945); 62:5 (May 1945); 62:8 (August 1945); 62:11 (November 1945); 67:3 (March 1950); 67:6 (June 1950); 67:9 (September 1950); 67:12 (December 1950); 72:1 (January 1955); 72:4 (April 1955); 72:7 (July 1955); 72:10 (October 1955); 77:2 (February 1960); 77:5 (May 1960); 77:8 (August 1960); 77:11 (November 1960).

Saturday Evening Post (Philadelphia: Curtis Publishing Co.): 182:27 (January 1, 1910); 182:28 (January 8, 1910); 182:29 (January 15, 1910); 182:30 (January 22, 1910); 182:40 (April 2, 1910); 182:41 (April 9, 1910); 182:42 (April 16, 1910); 182:43 (April 23, 1910); 183:1 (July 2, 1910); 183:2 (July 9, 1910); 183:3 (July 16, 1910); 183:4 (July 23, 1910); 183:14 (October 1, 1910); 183:15 (October 8, 1910); 183:16 (October 15, 1910); 183:17 (October 22, 1910); 187:32 (February 6, 1915); 187:33 (February 13, 1915); 187:34 (February 20, 1915); 187:35 (February 28, 1915); 187:44 (May 1, 1915); 187:45 (May 8, 1915); 187:46 (May 16, 1915); 187:47 (May 23, 1915); 188:6 (August 7, 1915); 188:7 (August 14, 1915); 188:8 (August 21, 1915); 188:9 (August 28, 1915); 188:19 (November 6, 1915); 188:20 (November 13, 1915); 188:21 (November 20, 1915); 188:22 (November 27, 1915); 192:36 (March 6, 1920); 192:37 (March 13, 1920); 192:38 (March 20, 1920); 192:39 (March 27, 1920); 192:49 (June 5, 1920); 192:50 (June 12, 1920); 192:51 (June 19, 1920); 192:52 (June 26, 1920); 193:10 (September 4, 1920); 193:11 (September 11, 1920); 193:12 (September 18, 1920); 193:13 (September 25, 1920); 193:23 (December 4, 1920); 193:24 (December 11, 1920); 193:25 (December 18, 1920); 193:26 (December 25, 1920); 197:27 (January 3, 1925); 197:28 (January 10, 1925); 197:29 (January 17, 1925); 197:30 (January 24, 1925); 197:40 (April 4, 1925); 197:41 (April 11, 1925); 197:42 (April 18, 1925); 197:43 (April 25, 1925); 198:1 (July 4, 1925); 198:2 (July 11, 1925); 198:3 (July 16, 1925); 198:4 (July 23, 1925); 198:14 (October 3, 1925); 198:15 (October 10, 1925); 198:16 (October 17, 1925); 198:17 (October 24, 1925); 202:31 (February 1, 1930); 202:32 (February 8, 1930); 202:33 (February 15, 1930); 202:34 (February 22, 1930); 202:44 (May 3, 1930); 202:45 (May 10, 1930); 202:46 (May 17, 1930); 202:47 (May 24, 1930); 203:6 (August 2, 1930); 203:7 (August 9, 1930); 203:8 (August 16, 1930); 203:9 (August 23, 1930); 203:18 (November 1, 1930); 203:19 (November 8, 1930); 203:20

(November 15, 1930); 203:21 (November 22, 1930); 207:35 (March 2, 1935); 207:36 (March 9, 1935); 207:37 (March 16, 1935); 207:38 (March 23, 1935); 207:48 (June 1, 1935); 207:49 (June 8, 1935); 207:50 (June 15, 1935); 207:51 (June 22, 1935); 208:10 (September 7, 1935); 208:11 (September 14, 1935); 208:12 (September 21, 1935); 208:13 (September 28, 1935); 208:23 (December 7, 1935); 208:24 (December 14, 1935); 208:25 (December 21, 1935); 208:26 (December 28, 1935); 212:28 (January 6, 1940); 212:29 (January 13, 1940); 212:30 (January 20, 1940); 212:31 (January 27, 1940); 212:41 (April 6, 1940); 212:42 (April 13, 1940); 212:43 (April 20, 1940); 212:44 (April 27, 1940); 213:1 (July 6, 1940); 213:2 (July 13, 1940); 213:3 (July 20, 1940); 213:4 (July 27, 1940); 213:14 (October 5, 1940); 213:15 (October 12, 1940); 213:16 (October 19, 1940); 213:17 (October 26, 1940); 217:32 (February 3, 1945); 217:33 (February 10, 1945); 217:34 (February 17, 1945); 217:35 (February 24, 1945); 217:45 (May 5, 1945); 217:46 (May 12, 1945); 217:47 (May 19, 1945); 217:48 (May 26, 1945); 218:5 (August 5, 1945); 218:6 (August 12, 1945); 218:7 (August 19, 1945); 218:8 (August 26, 1945); 218:18 (November 3, 1945); 218:19 (November 10, 1945); 218:20 (November 17, 1945); 218:21 (November 24, 1945); 222:32 (February 4, 1950); 222:33 (February 11, 1950); 222:34 (February 18, 1950); 222:35 (February 25, 1950); 222:45 (May 6, 1950); 222:46 (May 13, 1950); 222:47 (May 20, 1950); 222:48 (May 27, 1950); 223:6 (August 5, 1950); 223:7 (August 12, 1950); 223:8 (August 19, 1950); 223:9 (August 26, 1950); 223:19 (November 4, 1950); 223:20 (November 11, 1950); 223:21 (November 18, 1950); 223:22 (November 25, 1950); 227:36 (March 5, 1955); 227:37 (March 12, 1955); 227:38 (March 19, 1955); 227:39 (March 26, 1955); 227:49 (June 4, 1955); 227:50 (June 11, 1955); 227:51 (June 18, 1955); 227:52 (June 25, 1955); 228:10 (September 3, 1955); 228:11 (September 10, 1955); 228:12 (September 17, 1955); 228:13 (September 24, 1955); 228:23 (December 3, 1955); 228:24 (December 10, 1955); 228:25 (December 17, 1955); 228:26 (December 24, 1955); 232:27 (January 2, 1960); 232:28 (January 9, 1960); 232:29 (January 16, 1960); 232:30 (January 23, 1960); 232:40 (April 2, 1960); 232:41 (April 9, 1960); 232:42 (April 16, 1960); 232:43 (April 23, 1960); 233:1 (July 5, 1960); 233:2 (July 12, 1960); 233:3 (July 19, 1960); 233:4 (July 26, 1960); 233:14 (October 1, 1960); 233:15 (October 8, 1960); 233:16 (October 15, 1960); 233:17 (October 22, 1960).

Bibliography

Primary Sources

"The Committee of 50 on Journalism." *Bulletin, Home Economic Association* 5:4 (December 1916): 68–69.

"Declaration of Sentiments and Resolutions." Adopted by the Seneca Falls Convention, July 19–120, 1848. Reprinted in *Available Means: An Anthology of Women's Rhetoric(s),* ed. Joy Ritchie and Kate Ronald, 138–42. Pittsburgh: University of Pittsburgh Press, 2001.

Farm Magazines, Milestones, and Memories: American Agricultural Editors' Association, 1921–1996. New Prague, Minn.: AAEA, 1996.

Goss, Leonarda. "Planning My Magazine." *Bulletin, Home Economic Association* 5:4 (December 1916): 86–88.

Helder, Helen. *In One Lifetime.* Iowa City: The Printing House, 1992.

Hines, Stephen W., ed. *Laura Ingalls Wilder, Farm Journalist: Writings from the Ozarks.* Columbia: University of Missouri Press, 2007.

Holtz, William, ed. *Dorothy Thompson and Rose Wilder Lane: Forty Years of Friendship: Letters, 1921–1960.* Columbia: University of Missouri Press, 1991.

———. *Travels with Zenobia: Paris to Albania by Model T. Ford: A Journal by Rose Wilder Lane and Helen Dore Boylston.* Columbia: University of Missouri Press, 1983.

Lane, Rose Wilder. "American Enters Jerusalem." *Ladies' Home Journal* 36 (April 1919): 7–8.

———. "Behind the Headlight." *San Francisco Bulletin,* October 9–November 5, 1915.

———. "Behind the Screens in Movie Land." *San Francisco Bulletin,* October 25–December 12, 1917.

———. "The Big Break at Folsom." *San Francisco Bulletin,* January 4–February 1, 1917.

———. "A Bit of Gray in a Blue Sky." *Ladies' Home Journal* 36 (August 1919).

———. "The Building of Hetch-Hetchy." *San Francisco Bulletin,* October 4–November 14, 1916.

———. "The City at Night." *San Francisco Bulletin,* April 30–May 16, 1917.

———. *The Discovery of Freedom: Man's Struggle against Authority.* 1936. Reprint. Foreword by Jon Lefevre. New York: Arno Press, 1972.

———. *Diverging Roads.* New York: Century, 1919.

———. "Ed Monroe, Manhunter." *San Francisco Bulletin,* August 11–September 15, 1915.

———. *Give Me Liberty.* New York: Longmans, Green and Co., 1936.

———. "If I Could Live My Life Over Again." *Cosmopolitan* 78 (March 1925): 32.

———. "Innocence." *Harper's* 144 (April 1922): 577–84.

———. "The Insidious Enemy." *Good Housekeeping* 71:6 (December 1920).

———. "I, Rose Wilder Lane . . ." *Cosmopolitan* 79 (June 1926): 42.

———. "Life and Jack London." *Sunset,* October 1917–1918.

———. "Mother No. 22,999." *Good Housekeeping* 70:3 (March 1920).

———. *Old Home Town.* New York: Longmans, Green, 1935.

———. "Out of Prison." *San Francisco Bulletin,* February 2–March 15, 1917.

———. "Out of the East Christ Came." *Good Housekeeping* 69:5 (November 1919).

———. *Peaks of Shala.* New York: Harper, 1923.

———. "Rose Lane Says." *Pittsburgh Courier,* April 3, 1943.

———. "Rose Wilder Lane, by Herself." *Sunset* 41 (November 1918): 26.

———. "Soldiers of the Soil." *San Francisco Bulletin,* February 23\June 3, 1916.

———. *The Story of Art Smith.* San Francisco: Bulletin, 1915.

———. "Strange as Foreign Places." *McCalls* 49 (September 1919).

———. "World Travelogue." *San Francisco Call and Bulletin,* April 10, 1938.

Wilder, Laura Ingalls. *A Little House Reader.* Ed. William Anderson. New York: HarperCollins, 1998.

———. *A Little House Sampler.* Ed. William Anderson. New York: HarperCollins, 1988.

———. *West from Home: Letters of Laura Ingalls Wilder San Francisco, 1915.* Ed. Roger Lea MacBride. New York: HarperCollins, 1974.

Secondary Sources

Abrahamson, David. *Magazine-Made America: The Cultural Transformation of the Postwar Periodical.* Cresskill, N.J.: Hampton Press, 1996.

Adams, Jane. "The *Farm Journal*'s Discourse of Farm Women's Femininity." *Anthropology and Humanism* 29:1 (June 2004): 45–62.

Allin, Bushrod W. "The U.S. Department of Agriculture as an Instrument of Public Policy: In Retrospect and in Prospect." *Journal of Farm Economics* 42:5 (December 1960): 1094–1103.

Anderson, Benedict, *Imagined Communities: Reflections on the Origin and Spread of Nationalism.* Rev. ed. New York: Verso, 1991.

Anderson, William, ed. *Laura's Album: A Remembrance Scrapbook of Laura Ingalls Wilder.* New York: HarperCollins, 1998.

———. *The Little House Guidebook.* New York: HarperTrophy, 1996.

Armitage, Susan. "Here's to Women: Western Women Speak Up." *Journal of American History* 83:2 (September 1996): 551–59.

Beard, Mary Ritter. "Woman as Force in History: A Study in Traditions and Realities." In *Mary Ritter Beard: A Source Book,* ed. Ann J. Lane, 172–91. Boston: Northeastern University Press, 1977.

Beasley, Maurine H. "Women in Journalism: Contributors to Male Experience or Voices of Feminine Expression? How Historians Have Told the Stories of Women Journalists." *American Journalism* 7 (Winter 1990): 39–54.

Beasley, Maurine H., and Sheila J. Gibbons. *Taking Their Place: A Documentary History of Women and Journalism.* Washington, D.C.: American University Press, 1993.

Beasley, Maurine H., and Sheila Silver. *Women in Media: A Documentary Sourcebook.* Washington, D.C.: Women's Institute for Freedom of the Press, 1977.

Berger, Peter, and Thomas Luckmann. *The Social Construction of Reality: A Treatise in the Sociology of Knowledge.* Garden City, N.Y.: Doubleday, 1966.

Berkhofer, Robert F., Jr. "Narratives and Historicization." In *Beyond the Great Story: History as Text and Discourse,* 26–44. Cambridge: Belknap Press of Harvard University Press, 1995.

Blair, Emily Newell. "Women in the Political Parties." *Annals of the American Academy of Political and Social Science* 143 (May 1929): 217–29.

Carey, James. *Communication as Culture: Essays on Media and Society.* New York: Routledge, 1989.

Covert, Catherine L. "Journalism History and Women's Experience: A Problem in Conceptual Change." *Journalism History* 8:1 (Spring 1981): 2–6.

Cox, Sherilyn. "Women Suffrage Papers of the West, 1869–1914." *American Journalism* 3:3 (1987): 129–41.

Cramer, Janet M. "Woman as Citizen: Race, Class, and the Discourse of Women's Citizenship, 1894–1909." *Journalism and Mass Communication Monographs* 165 (March 1998).

Crane, Diana. "Introduction: The Challenge of the Sociology of Culture to Sociology as a Discipline." In *The Sociology of Culture,* 1–19. Cambridge, Mass.: Blackwell, 1994.

Damon-Moore, Helen. *Magazines for the Millions: Gender and Commerce in the "Ladies' Home Journal" and the "Saturday Evening Post," 1880–1910.* Albany: State University of New York Press, 1994.

Domhoff, G. William. "The Women's Page as Window on the Ruling Class." In *Hearth and Home: Images of Women in the Mass Media,* ed. Gaye Tuchman, Arlene Kaplan Daniels and James Benet, 161–75. New York: Oxford University Press, 1978.

Domke, David. "Journalists, Framing, and Discourse about Race Relations." *Journalism and Mass Communication Monographs* 164 (1997): 1.

Emery, Michael. "The Writing of American Journalism History." *Journalism History* 10:3–4 (Autumn/Winter 1983): 39–43.

Enstad, Nan. *Ladies of Labor, Girls of Adventure: Working Women, Popular Culture, and Labor Politics at the Turn of the Twentieth Century.* New York: Columbia University Press, 1999.

Fairclough, Norman. *Discourse and Social Change.* Cambridge, UK: Polity Press, 1992.

———. *Media Discourse.* London: Edward Arnold, 1995.

Faragher, John Mack. "History from the Inside-Out: Writing the History of Women in Rural America." *American Quarterly* 33:5 (Winter 1981): 537–57.

Foner, Eric. *The Story of American Freedom.* New York: W. W. Norton and Co., 1998.

Fox, Bonnie J. "Selling the Mechanized Household: 70 years of Ads in Ladies' Home Journal." *Gender and Society* 4:1 (March 1990): 25–40.

Fraser, Steve, and Gary Gerstle, eds. *The Rise and Fall of the New Deal Order.* Princeton: Princeton University Press, 1989.

Freshwater, David. "Farm Production Policy versus Rural Life Policy." *American Journal of Agricultural Economics* 79:5 (December 1997): 1515–24.

Friedberger, Mark. *Farm Families and Change in Twentieth-Century America.* Lexington: University Press of Kentucky, 1988.

Ginzberg, Lori D. "Re-Viewing the First Wave." *Feminist Studies* 28:2 (Summer 2002): 419–34.

Grace, Margaret, and June Lennie. "Constructing and Reconstructing Rural Women in Australia: The Politics of Change, Diversity and Identity." *Sociologia Ruralis* 38:3 (1998): 351–70.

Gregory, James N. *American Exodus: The Dust Bowl Migration and Okie Culture in California.* New York: Oxford University Press, 1989.

Hall, Stuart. "Encoding, Decoding." In *The Cultural Studies Reader,* ed. Simon During, 507–17. 2d ed. New York: Routledge, 1999.

Helmbold, Lois Rita, and Ann Schofield. "Women's Labor History." *Reviews in American History* 17:4 (December 1989): 501–18.

Hilliard, Sam B. "The Dynamics of Power: Recent Trends in Mechanization on the American Farm." *Technology and Culture* 12:1 (January, 1972): 1–24.

Hines, Stephen W., ed. *I Remember Laura: America's Favorite Storyteller as Remembered by Her Family, Friends, and Neighbors.* Nashville: Thomas Nelson, 1994.

Hodgson, Godfrey. *America in Our Time.* New York: Vintage Books, 1976.

Hoffschwelle, Mary S. "'Better Homes on Better Farms': Domestic Reform in Rural Tennessee." *Frontiers: A Journal of Women's Studies* 22:1 (2001): 51–73.

Holtz, William. *The Ghost in the Little House: A Life of Rose Wilder Lane.* Columbia: University of Missouri Press, 1993.

Horowitz, Daniel. "Rethinking Betty Friedan and *The Feminist Mystique:* Labor Union Radicalism and Feminism in Cold War America." *American Quarterly* 48:1 (1996): 1–42.

Jenkins, Henry. *Textual Poachers.* New York: Routledge, 1992.

Jensen, Joan M. "'I'd Rather Be Dancing': Wisconsin Women Moving On." *Frontiers: A Journal of Women's Studies* 22:1 (2001): 1–20.

———. *Promise to the Land: Essays on Rural Women.* Albuquerque: University of New Mexico Press, 1991.

———. *With These Hands.* New York: Feminist Press at CUNY, 1981.

Jensen, Joan M., and Anne B. W. Effland. "Introduction." *Frontiers: A Journal of Women's Studies* 22:1 (2001): iii–xvii.

Kaestle, Carl. *Literacy in the United States: Readers and Reading since 1880.* New Haven: Yale University Press, 1991.

Kerber, Linda. "Separate Spheres, Female Worlds, Woman's Place: The Rhetoric of Women's History." In *Toward an Intellectual History of Women,* 159–99. Chapel Hill: University of North Carolina Press, 1997.

Kessler-Harris, Alice. *In Pursuit of Equity: Women, Men, and the Quest for Economic Citizenship in 20th-Century America.* New York: Oxford University Press, 2001.

———. *Out to Work: A History of Wage-Earning Women in the United States, 20th Anniversary Edition.* New York: Oxford University Press, 2003.

———. *Women Have Always Worked.* New York: McGraw Hill, 1981.

Kitch, Carolyn. *The Girl on the Magazine Cover: The Origins of Visual Stereotypes in American Mass Media.* Chapel Hill: University of North Carolina Press, 2001.

Kress, Gunther. "Ideological Structures in Discourse." In *Handbook of Discourse Analysis, Volume 4, Discourse Analysis in Society,* ed. Teun A. van Dijk, 27–42. London: Academic Press, 1985.

Leiserson, Avery. "Opinion Research and the Political Process: Farm Policy as an Example." *Public Opinion Quarterly* 13:1 (Spring 1949): 31–38.

Leonard, Thomas C. *News for All: America's Coming of Age with the Press.* New York, Oxford: Oxford University Press, 1995.

Lyson, Thomas A. "Husband and Wife Work Roles and the Organization and Operation of Family Farms." *Journal of Marriage and Family* 47:3 (August 1985): 759–64.

Mather, Anne. "A History of Feminist Periodicals, Part I." *Journalism History* 1:3 (Autumn 1974): 82–85.

———. "A History of Feminist Periodicals, Part II." *Journalism History* 1:4 (Winter 1974–1975): 108–11.

May, Elaine Tyler. *Homeward Bound: American Families in the Cold War Era.* Rev. ed. New York: Basic Books, 1999.

McCullough, David. *John Adams.* New ed. New York: Simon and Schuster, 2008.

Meiners, Jane E., and Geraldine I. Olson. "Household, Paid, and Unpaid Work Time of Farm Women." *Family Relations* 36:4 (October 1987): 407–11.

Miller, John E. *Becoming Laura Ingalls Wilder: The Woman behind the Legend.* Columbia: University of Missouri Press, 1998.

Mills, Kay. *A Place in the News: From the Women's Pages to the Front Page.* New York: Columbia University Press, 1990.

Mitchell, Catherine C. "The Place of Biography in the History of News Women: What Role Should Biographical Research Play in Writing the History of Women Journalists?" *American Journalism* 7 (Winter 1990): 23–32.

Newcomb, Horace M. "On the Dialogic Aspects of Mass Communication." *Critical Studies in Mass Communication* 1 (1984): 34–50.

Nord, David Paul. *Communities of Journalism.* Urbana and Chicago: University of Illinois Press, 2001.

Norris, Pippa, ed. *Women, Media and Politics.* New York and Oxford: Oxford University Press, 1997.

Oldrup, Helene. "Women Working off the Farm: Reconstruction Gender Identity in Danish Agriculture." *Sociologia Ruralis* 39:3 (1998): 343–58.

Pettersen, Liv Toril, and Hilde Solbakken. "Empowerment as a Strategy for Change for Farm Women in Western Industrialized Countries." *Sociologia Ruralis* 38:3 (1998): 318–30.

Rahman, Atiqur, and John Westley. "The Challenge of Ending Rural Poverty." *Development Policy Review* 19:4 (2001): 553–62.

Rogers, Susan. "Female Forms of Power and the Myth of Male Dominance: A Model of Female-Male Interaction in Peasant Society." *American Ethnologist* 2 (1975): 727–56.

Romines, Ann. *Constructing the Little House: Gender, Culture, and Laura Ingalls Wilder.* Amherst: University of Massachusetts Press, 1997.

Rosenfeld, Rachel Ann. *Farm Women: Work, Farm, and Family in the United States.* Chapel Hill: University of North Carolina Press, 1985.

Sachs, Carolyn E. *Invisible Farmers: Women in Agricultural Production.* Totowa, N.J.: Roman and Allanheld, 1983.

Scott, Joan Wallach. "The Problem of Invisibility." In *Retrieving Women's History,* ed. S. Jay Kleinberg, 5–29. New York: Berg/UNESCO, 1988.

Shortall, Sally. *Women and Farming: Property and Power.* London: Macmillan, 1999.

Simon, Rita J., and Gloria Danziger. *Women's Movements in America: Their Successes, Disappointments, and Aspirations.* New York: Praeger, 1991.

Sloan, William. *American Journalism History: An Annotated Bibliography.* New York: Greenwood Press, 1989.

Solomon, Martha M., ed. *A Voice of Their Own: The Woman Suffrage Press, 1840–1910.* Tuscaloosa: University of Alabama Press, 1991.

Steeves, H. Leslie. "Feminist Theories and Media Studies." *Critical Studies in Mass Communication* 4 (1987): 95–135.

Stone, Kathryn H. "Women as Citizens." *Annals of the American Academy of Political and Social Science* 251 (May 1947): 79–86.

Storey, John. "Introduction." In *What Is Cultural Studies? A Reader,* 1–13. New York: Arnold Publishing, 1996.

Susman, Warren I. *Culture as History: The Transformation of American Society in the Twentieth Century.* New York: Pantheon Books, 1984.

Tanner, Bonnie O. *The Entrepreneurial Characteristics of Farm Women.* New York: Garland Publishing, 1999.

Thompson, Paul B., and Thomas C. Hilde. *The Agrarian Roots of Pragmatism.* Nashville: Vanderbilt University Press, 2000.

Tuchman, Gaye. *Making News: A Study in the Construction of Reality.* New York: Free Press, 1978.

———. "The Newspaper as a Social Movement's Resource." In *Hearth and Home: Images of Women in the Mass Media,* ed. Gaye Tuchman, Arlene Kaplan Daniels, and James Benet, 186–215. New York: Oxford University Press, 1978.

Ulrich, Laurel Thatcher. *A Midwife's Tale: The Life of Martha Ballard, Based on Her Diary, 1785–1812.* New York: Vintage, 1991.

Van Dijk, Teun A. "Media Contents: The Interdisciplinary Study of News as Discourse." In *A Handbook of Qualitative Methodologies for Mass Communication Research,* ed. Klaus Bruhn Jensen and Nicholas W. Jankowski, 108–19. New York: Routledge, 1991.

Walker, Nancy A. "The *Ladies' Home Journal,* 'How America Lives' and the Limits of Cultural Diversity." *Media History* 6:2 (February 2000): 129–38.

———. *Shaping Our Mothers' World: American Women's Magazines.* Jackson: University Press of Mississippi, 2000.

———. *Women's Magazines, 1940–1960: Gender Roles and the Popular Press.* Boston: Bedford/St. Martins, 1998.

Welter, Barbara. "The Cult of True Womanhood." *American Quarterly* 18 (Summer 1966): 151–74.

Whatmore, Sarah. *Farming Women: Gender, Work, and Family Enterprise.* London: Macmillan, 1991.

Zuckerman, Mary Ellen. *A History of Popular Women's Magazines in the United States, 1792–1995.* Westport, Conn.: Greenwood Press, 1998.

Dissertations, Theses, and Unpublished Articles

Canaday, Margot. "Children, Crops, Canning, and Communism: The Intersection of Family and Politics in the Personal Narrative of Agrarian Radical Lena Borchardt." Paper submitted for American studies course, University of Minnesota, Winter 1997.

Cash, K. W. "The Relationship between Rural Prosperity and Circulation and Advertising in Farm Magazines." B.S. thesis, Iowa State College, 1927.

Lauters, Amy Mattson. "The Voice of *The Farmer's Wife:* Wife, Mother, Citizen, Businesswoman, 1911–1926." Paper, American Journalism Historians Association annual conference, Billings, Mont., October 2003.

———. "'We Are Legion': Community-Building and *The Farmer's Wife,* 1955–1962." Paper, American Journalism Historians Association annual conference, San Antonio, Tex., October 2005.

———. "'Why Should I Stay?': Rural Woman's Voice through Laura Ingalls Wilder, 1911–1926." Paper, American Journalism Historians Association annual conference, Nashville, Tenn., October 2002.

Reber, Norman Franklin. "Main Factors That Influence the Editorial Content of Farm Magazines." Ph.D. diss., University of Pennsylvania, 1960.

Ward, Douglas B. "Barbarians, Farmers, and Consumers: Curtis Publishing Company and the Search for Rural America, 1910–1930." Paper, American Journalism Historians Association convention, Cleveland, Ohio, October 2004.

Index